Older Women Don't Giggle

Memoirs of a Renaissance Man

K Charles Oelfke 2nd

The Reading Glass Books
1-888-420-3050
www.readingglassbooks.com
fulfillment@readingglassbooks.com

Table of Contents

To my dear wife Josefa, who said, when I began writing;
"I'm not concerned with your past;
I'm only concerned with your future."

Introduction

Once in a while you see one—striking, intriguing, sure of herself, sometimes even breathtaking. She radiates *that certain something,* which can best be described as *fascinating* - exuding sex at every step.

She is *la femme d'un certain âge,* as the French refer to a woman of indeterminate age who is sophisticated and attractive. How elegant a phrase, and not at all derogatory. Indeed, it can imply an undercurrent of mystery, combined with a certain fascination and respect for the lady so described. From here on, I will refer to them as FCA's and it will *always* be used as a complimentary term.

In English we have no comparable expression (maybe because we have no comparable women?). Anglo-Saxon society seems unable to recognize or even to admit the existence of the excitement that smolders in these women, just waiting for a breath of interest to provoke it into flame.

"Middle-aged woman?" How unflattering. Why does our English expression conjure up visions of dowdy, plain clothes and sensible shoes? Maybe it's because these women in our Puritan-based society tend to think of themselves that way, so they simply accept the role and act accordingly.

Words tend to follow ideas, like form follows function. The Anglo-Saxon mind simply isn't interested in (or maybe it's the Puritan mind that won't let it see) the wonderful potential for sexual love and latent, explosive animal lust hidden within these women.

Nature is only interested in reproduction; the preservation of the race. Start reproducing at the onset of puberty and then slink off quietly into the sunset. So don't look to nature for guidance. Past the reproductive years, women are ready for the dustbin. Nature is no longer concerned with what happens to them - they have served their purpose.

Society, on the other hand, seems to have been structured in contradiction to what nature wants. The *woman of a certain age,* according to our outdated cultural rules, was supposed to have had one mate (another word for marriage), had only one man in her bed (her husband), and stopped thinking about sex when she stopped reproducing. Since the sexual revolution though, young girls don't hesitate to have multiple partners. But just wait and see how neglected they become when they reach that *certain age.*

The most destructive influence on sex after forty five is *marriage.* The second most destructive influence is simply the basic difference between men and women.

Married as virgins? Probably not in this day and age, though many of today's FCAs may have. In any case, they began their sex lives as bungling beginners, followed by twenty years of boring sex and raising children. Sex often got off to a lousy start in the back seat of a car, a cheap motel, or a desert beer party, and guilt or pregnancy set in, which was why many young people got married in the first place.

But that's the way it *used* to be. Now cars are smaller and morals are broader. Things may be easier and more open, but from what I've seen, the quality of sex has not improved.

There are more women disappointed in sex in general, and later-life sex in particular, than there are satisfied customers. Most women will tell you that their first experience with sexual intercourse was very disappointing, painful, and uninteresting. And often times it went downhill from there. According to research psychologist Ellen Frank, even well-functioning couples said sex with them ranged from so-so to outright failure 10 percent of the time, and that mutual satisfaction is reached only 40 percent of the time at best.

Now that we have easy access to material on the subject (Masters and Johnson, Hite, *Cosmopolitan* magazine), women are reading about how sex should or could be and... *the natives are restless!*

Today, she knows what she is missing. Of course she's frustrated. She keeps it to herself, reads romance novels, and fantasizes about sexual encounters of the earth shattering kind. The covers of romance novels always seem to illustrate the same scenario. One cover illustration could be exchanged for any other. He is handsome, shirtless, muscular, and arching over her (dominating), while she is lower in the picture, arching backward (submissive) with bodice askew. What might be mistaken for forced sex is readily understood by every woman as being the romantic, unknown "knight in shining armor who is sweeping me off my feet, tearing my bodice, and since I can't resist, *I am not to blame*" that populates her fantasies. Guilt is kept out of the scenario. Women say, when discussing their dreams, that the dream lover is always a faceless unknown. By not choosing the partner (through recognition), the sexual encounter remains fantasy, more exciting, with less reason to feel guilt.

Men? They're *always* satisfied. With a beautiful woman, with a homely woman, after a couple of drinks, with two slices of liver in a radiator, or a jar of peanut butter, or one hand on the remote and one hand on *it*. It always works and never fails. He's a selfish Monday night couch potato who has long ago lost concern for satisfying his wife in bed. Satisfying *himself*, of course remains important, but he can do that blindfolded with his head in a bucket.

Men and women are different — *very different.*
We all know it.
We all recognize it. Men can explain it.
Women *understand* the explanation, but they can't accept it.

In fact, men use it as an excuse for their infidelities.

Women have a real problem with it. They admit that they know men are different, but that doesn't mean they are willing to accept the difference.

Women are, by nature, monogamous nesters; men, by nature, are not. Men want sex with multiple partners, but society pressures them into selecting *one* woman with whom to "settle down" and have a family. Simple isn't it?

No it isn't.

When a man makes the *settle down* decision, he is announcing to his world *that he will never touch another woman for the rest of his life* ("until death do us part," remember?).

How many men really think about that promise deep in their groins when they decide, blinded by that "love" thing, to marry?

When we say "by nature," we mean that nature made us that way. (Remember what I said earlier. Nature has only one purpose - the propagation of the race, or reproduction.) Nature was smart - make it pleasurable so they'll want to do it all the time. Men were given the means of impregnating many, many females. Women were given the responsibility of bearing as many offspring as possible. Nature knew that, if it *hurt*, no one would do it. So nature filled men and women with hormones and made it feel *sooo good* that they would think of little else.

Society tries to bend nature to its ever-changing manners and mores, but it just doesn't work. Nature says procreation begins at puberty. Society says, "No! No!" first you must finish school, find a job, find a partner for life, and then get married and have children - blah, blah, blah. We love to make these moral laws about when people can date, when they can marry, how old the partner can be, and so on. Mothers start pimping for their daughters, trying to couple them up with Mr. Right, which means "a good catch," which really means the right Ivy League school, family connections, societal standing.

Think about this. (I don't know to whom I should give credit; probably a stand-up comedian) "Men talk to women so woman will go to bed with them; women go to bed with men so men will talk to them."

Men depend on visual stimuli. ("Let's leave the light on, and put on your black teddy.") Women depend on *spoken* stimuli. ("Let's turn the light off, and tell me you love me.") By the time a man has seen the same woman naked every day for twenty-five years plus, it is understandable that it's going to take something more to visually excite him. This has nothing at all to do with his *feelings* for her. He may love her deeply, but she begins to feel ashamed of her body because it no longer produces the effect it used to. She realizes that the mere sight of her upper thigh is no longer cause for an immediate erection.

He's looking over the fence at the neighbor in shorts (whose thighs are not *better*, they're just *newer)* or having it off with his secretary while home sex dies on the vine. But he still loves her and would be lost if she left. Try to make her understand.

Self-blame sets in.

"If he really loved me, he wouldn't need to look at *Playboy* or internet porn."

"If he really loved me, he would want me more often (even though he seldom satisfies me). But that new pool boy sure is cute."

So just when they could blossom into FCAs, they are neglected-just when their needs, appetites, and sexual potential are at their peaks. It is also the period in their lives when they can be the most exciting, intriguing and desirable-if they can just find that potential within themselves, understand it, and exploit it.

Some women have it; some women don't.

But now we face the real problem.

It is too late for the husband of many years to become "reactivated" to this woman. We read in women's magazines that it's never too late to "put spice back in the bedroom." Some version of this claim is almost always featured on the cover of *Ladies' Home Journal*. This subject is never talked about in *Game and Fish*, *Motor Sport*, or *Car and Driver* magazines. Think about it. We know that rarely works. Even *trying* to relight the cigar is often ridiculous and embarrassing for both parties. He is in need of new stimulation, new fantasies, new sex objects, or a different woman. And so, in fact, is she. So how about a different man?

One solution used by many couples is watching erotic films together. Another solution is for them to accept an arrangement where they are each free to find (discreetly of course) satisfaction outside the marriage. The danger here is that as I often say, "a satisfied woman is a woman in love."

Now is the time for the woman to turn to younger men. A pussy is a terrible thing to waste.

"Oh my, *No!* I could *never* go to bed with a younger man." "*Goodness* no. I could never do that. No! No! *Never!*"

She believes that is the way she feels. But in fact, that's just the way she *thinks* she should feel. She's simply expressing a conditioned reaction. Underneath, her subconscious continues thinking, *He's young enough to be my son, so by association I would be committing some terrible blah, blah, blah.*

I have been involved with many, I should say *only* FCAs. And every one of them, without fail, would have adamantly denied any possibility of ever becoming involved with a man twenty to thirty years her junior.

But they all did just that.

Once a relationship is under way and the FCA is comfortable with it, she will invariably say, "I still don't understand how it happened."

"I never would have believed it could happen to me." "I never saw *that* coming."

That is simply her conditioned conscience speaking. In reality, she is feeling a bit giddy and pleased with herself yet not quite sure what or how it happened - like a high jumper who has just broken a world record.

(We'll deal with *how* it happened later on, because it does *not* just happen by chance.)

She will go through a period of wondering; what will my friends think? What would my children think? until she realizes that at least her girlfriends are all envious as hell and wishing they had the courage to do the same thing. They are stuck with their couch potatoes while *she* is looking radiant with a new sparkle in her eye and a lilt in her walk. It takes some time for her to accept that she has every right to the relationship. She has a partner with a comparable sex drive and a desire to please, who thinks she's beautiful and who appreciates what she has to offer. I've heard said that "a desired body is a beautiful body." He's found a partner who hungers for his sexual vigor and can help him become an expert lover, deal with adult situations, and mature comfortably.

It will be a while before she's ready to let her family know about the relationship. She doesn't know how long it will last, afraid it won't last. She's afraid of looking foolish, and she knows that society would frown and call her names. Her children won't know how to deal with the competition, for that is just what her lover is to them - competition for her affections; her time; and often, in their minds anyway, her money. It's nothing more than sibling jealousy

That is something I would like to see change. A man can date a young girl, and that's okay. Her pimping mother loves the idea that her daughter has found someone with money to take care of her (read: "sugar daddy," doctor, lawyer, and so on). So why can't FCAs have affairs with young men without being sought out by Oprah or Phil?

Just like the older man with a younger woman, financial security plays a role. Money shouldn't be a problem because the mature woman is either a widow living on whatever her late husband left for her or a married woman whose husband takes care of her needs *except* sexually. These are the very women who are vulnerable to the tender innocence of a lusty young lover.

Once in a while, a film is made about an older woman with a younger man, but I have yet to see an honest story that is not afraid to tackle the subject head-on. *Summer of '42* was a disappointment. The story of a young boy with a woman in her twenties doesn't begin to do it, but I guess it was safe with the American public, and the woman was provided with an excuse - a justification for her actions. But I'm talking about a young man from eighteen to twenty-five years of age with a woman *at least forty*. Now that's an age difference to which I can relate. Women pass through a very *un*interesting phase between their late teens and late thirties. They are no longer young girls (which, as far as I'm concerned, are of little interest), but they have a long way to go before becoming an FCA. The typical mid- thirties woman is still trying to sort out her love life. Maybe married once and divorced or racing the biological clock, she's seeking a commitment from some guy who is so wary, he wears running shoes to bed. Women of that age have one foot in the sexual revolution; the other is trying to build a nest. Total panic!

To be avoided at all cost.

A woman does not become interesting until she matures in body and mind. At forty, women *begin* to merit a watchful eye. Remember too, that women reach their sexual peak much later than men. Some studies are now saying that peak is around sixty on up, and I believe it because I have seen it. There is nothing more satisfying or beautiful in my eyes than to guide a sixty-year- old woman to experiencing multiple orgasms for the first time in her life; her eyes close, her jaws clench, and her lips curl as she is racked with escalating spasms of pure ecstasy, often followed by sobbing while descending from the pinnacle of pleasure, pleading, "Don't touch me please. I can't take any more."

I still chuckle when I recall Theo, in *The Goldfinch*, by Donna Tartt, saying, "She was my first inkling that women over forty — women not all that great- looking — could be sexy. There was something sultry and exciting and tough about her too, an animal strength, a purring, prowling quality when she was out of her heels and walking barefoot." Thoughts of a teenage boy – yet written by a woman novelist.

The sexual peak for a man is about age twenty, so we are left with about forty years of compromising. The problem for older women is, quite simply, a shortage of partners.

One summer afternoon in 1957, I was lounging in the sun at the Piscine d'Eligny in Paris. The Piscined d'Eligny was a swimming pool suspended between river barges floating in the Seine at the *quai* Anatole-France (left bank), across the Seine from the Tuileries. For many years, it was a center of summertime leisure in a city where people didn't have ready access to swimming pools. Yet this one was within eyesight of the National Assembly and the Place de la Concorde. I say, *was*, because it burned and sank several years later and was never rebuilt, to the consternation of traditional left-bank Parisians. During its heyday, it had its regular fashionable visitors such as (I have read) Louis Philippe, George Sand, Louis Aragon, Jean Marais, Grace Kelly, Errol Flynn, and so on. Many didn't come to swim; they came, rather, to lounge, smoke Gauloise cigarettes, and converse on the day's important topics. There were other floating swimming pools in the Seine River around Paris. It was an ingenious solution, greatly appreciated by the locals. One was named after American-born Josephine Baker, who became a French citizen, helped in the French Resistance during World War II, and was awarded both the *Croix de Guerre* and the *Legion d'Honneur* for her service. She was the darling of French society, performing regularly at the famous Folies Bergère.

More than just a swimming pool, the Piscine d'Eligny was a complex of colorful changing booths along the sides under a roof overhang supported by iron poles, a café at one end with a sundeck overlooking the pool, deck chairs, and loungers on towels. It had the turn-of-the-century, Victorian charm of Deauville — all made of much-painted wood. It was created in 1785 but was transformed many times over the years until the fifties when I went there. Stored away during the winter months, it reappeared each summer.

There were probably thirty or forty sunbathers sitting and lying around the pool and deck area, appreciative of the balmy Paris summer weather, when an extraordinary vision entered. She appeared to be at least in her sixties or perhaps more — a two-piece bathing suit, high-heeled wooden slip-ons, a hat, sunglasses, a bag, and a towel. *A vision!*

People stopped what they were doing and looked up. Books were lowered. Conversations paused. Women and men watched transfixed as she walked the length of the open pool area, her superb derriere rolling with each stride, haughty breasts bobbing in cadence as she walked. She was there to take her place in the sun. I felt a combination of admiration, longing, and pure animal excitement. I'm certain that fantasy images raced through the minds of every man, and perhaps some women, present that day, regardless of age.

It was not so much her beauty that attracted us — at least not in terms of professional model beauty. No, it was much deeper and much more complex than that. She radiated *femininity*. She exuded sensuality and experience. She was "woman" personified. She was ageless, a goddess. By having it all, she made age irrelevant. She was probably more attractive at that age than she had been in her younger days. She certainly provoked more heavy breathing than did all the young girls at the pool that day.

Who was she? Age? Who knows? Certainly well beyond sixty…or sixty five, maybe even seventy. Who cared? She might have been a *grande dame*, a housewife or maybe a prostitute taking the afternoon sun before her tour along the Rue St. Denis. She left it up to us to fantasize as we wished. I wonder if she realized or sensed the effect she had caused. How could she not know, with the assurance she exuded? A vision that arrived from nowhere, she then disappeared, leaving many of us with one more fantasy for our memory banks, to be called upon when needed to help push us over the edge of a stubborn orgasm with a ho-hum partner. That was over sixty years ago, but I remember her in great detail to this day.

Had she been fully dressed, her clothing might have helped us define her. People's dress expresses personality, economic standing, and taste (or lack of taste); in some cases, perhaps even profession is suggested. But she was dressed for the beach, and that was more than enough for us that day.

Wherever she is, I wish she could know how she made my day that particular day.

My reason for introducing my book in this way is to make you, the reader, know from the beginning that I look at life from a different perspective than most other men do — particularly where women are concerned. As you will see as we take this journey together, I have lived an extraordinary life full of adventure, business experiences, travel, and excitement, interspersed with marvelous romantic, erotic experiences, which I will be more than happy to share with you.

Je Sait Bien, 1997

Et la nuit prend place au soleil pour toujours,
mon désir, ô comme je rêve.
Qu'import que Dieu clôt mon histoire.

Les souvenirs girent dans ma tête.
Mais soyez certain mon Coeur,
Apres tout, l'amour n'est qu'un rêve.
Nos rêves disait, souvenez-vous?
Elle êst partie, sans rien dire.
Je l'ai perdu; je l'ai perdu et pourtant
Pourtant elle etait la,
Puise-je espérer de la revoir?
Dieu, vous avez clos mon histoire.
Que puis-je faire? Elle est perdu?
Aprés tout, les larmes tiède

C'est plutôt moi qui est perdu.
Mais je l'ai bien perdu pourtant,
Elle s'enfui comme une mouette.
C'est plus fort que moi, voyez vous.
Mais la vie, c'est comme çela
Car, moineau, je sait bien. …je sait bien.

I Know Well

And the night replaces the sun forever,
My Desire, oh how I dream,
No matter that God closed my story.

Memories spin in my head.
But be certain my Heart,
After all, love is but a dream.
As our dreams said. Don't you remember?
She left, without a word.
I lost her; I lost her, and yet
And yet she was there.
Can I hope to see her again?
God, you have closed my story.
What can I do? She is lost?
After all the warm tears

It is rather I who is lost.
However, I have lost her nevertheless.
She fled like a kittiwake.
It's too much for me, you see
But life itself is that way.
Because, little sparrow,

I know well. I understand.

Chapter 1

Once Upon a Time

O nce upon a time, I met a femme d'un certain âge (FCA) who eventually became a good friend, though I hardly knew her at that time. She knew little about me—my past, hopes, whims, idiosyncrasies, or hang-ups. I guess she thought I was just a normal, if perhaps somewhat bent, individual, and I agree that was a fairly close description of who I am to this day.

One day, I was to drop off something at her house—I believe, if I remember correctly, a music CD that I thought she might appreciate. It was no big deal; I would stop my car, she would come out and pick up the disc, and that would be it—and it was. She had been working in her garden dressed in shorts and a T-shirt of sorts. The whole transaction took but a moment; I drove on.

Later, I telephoned to discuss her reaction to the music, the poetry of the songs, and the voice of the performer, an old favorite French composer and singer, who I had adored for years. She had not yet listened to the CD, so she couldn't comment on the music. But she was apologetic about her appearance when I stopped by—sweaty and dusty, a perfectly normal condition under the circumstances. Then she added, "I wasn't wearing a bra, so my nipples were showing."

I hemmed and hawed and muttered that I hadn't noticed (which I hadn't). It was all so quick. *Gee-zus!* Did I miss something?

That did it! Goodness me. How often does an attractive femme d'un certain âge mention her nipples in a casual conversation? The nipple image became lodged in my brain (nipple, nipple).

From then on, at every thought of her or her name, the word "nipple" screamed at me—silently, of course, as if some action were necessary. I remember an old Woody Allen movie in which he is being chased by a giant, bouncing breast. In some ways, it was intriguing and exciting: in other ways, it became haunting, even frightening. How could I have missed them? And now how could I make them stop?

You must understand. I had never seen, touched, caressed, fondled, or kissed them, and there was no chance that I ever would. But from that moment, I knew for certain that hers existed because she'd said they did. The idea had never entered my mind until that conversation. But now they took on a different reality altogether because she'd made them exist for me. They suddenly became real, and of course, a certain burgeoning lust was created in my mind over that one simple, innocent, but important word. She obviously had no idea what effect she had on me and probably would have laughed if she were to find out.

But she mustn't ever know.

"Men," she'd say. "They're so silly."

Chapter 2

The Body

The example I described is what every woman should strive for as she gains maturity and experience (in other words, as she approaches FCA potential). Yet many women seem to give up long before that. The successful passing of this threshold is dependent on a woman's state of mind — her attitude, not her beauty. If the attitude is positive, the attractiveness will follow. We all have among our friends at least one basically ordinary-looking woman who has such a delightfully appealing personality, that men hover about them like flies because they are attractive rather than beautiful. They have a certain *something*.

An attractive woman is a fascinating woman.

A beautiful woman is beautiful - *that's it*. But wait till she opens her mouth. Will that physical beauty transform into something more? Will she become attractive, fascinating? Not always.

Much responsibility lies with society's obsession with youth and youth only. After so many years of brainwashing in advertising, the older woman has been mentally forced to bow out, give up, go away, and "grow old gracefully."

On the other hand, not every woman is able to accept the challenge. Some women couldn't make it work no matter how hard they tried. This has nothing to do with age. Not all young girls are attractive either. Many of the young ones are not "sperm worthy." We're simply going to deal with those who are eager to take up the challenge - but they need our encouragement. They don't have to be beautiful in a classical sense. Every day, we see people getting married who could not be considered beautiful. Nature, to give everyone a chance, craftily complicated our lives further by inserting love into the equation. Such a move, for all intents and purposes, guarantees that there is someone for everyone out there somewhere.

Life, instead of taking a toll on women, can and should add to their attractiveness. Much of the problem comes from the woman herself. Very few think they are beautiful, pretty, or even attractive, even at an early age. A basic insecurity about looks seems to be built into the female mind. By the time they've produced and raised a few children on their way to reaching FCA status, they have low self-esteem about their looks, wrinkles, thighs, derrieres, necks, upper arms - but I could go on and on. This, of course, is what keeps the plastic surgeons in Beamers, Mercs, and Jags.

In a man's eye, a woman becomes the most desirable creature on earth at the moment he is about to bed her. Any woman, when lying naked on her back in anticipation of receiving her lover, seems to magically transform, becoming ever more beautiful in the eyes of her beholder. Women must learn to look at themselves less critically. Pamper your body; massage and caress it with oils and creams. That's what your lover will want to do.

You first must change these most basic negative attitudes and insecurities. To be sure, it takes work. It takes a positive outlook with intent to succeed. It means achieving a positive attitude that is three-quarters coquette and one-quarter femme fatale. An FCA should never try to act like the younger women she thinks are her competition. Those young women can't help acting the way they do, but the FCA certainly can; that's her great advantage. The older woman must always act her age, making that age desirable because the age she has is exactly the advantage she holds over the young, unsophisticated airheads. The only competition an FCA need fear is another FCA.

Potential FCAs must accept the following facts: cellulite can be sexy. Mature breasts are beautiful and very sexy. Laugh wrinkles around the eyes and mouth are beautiful and sexy. Avoid Botox, please, ladies. Those swollen puffy lips look ridiculous!

Because mature breasts and wrinkles around the eyes and mouths are living, natural parts of the FCA, they are sexy and exciting to anyone who has learned to appreciate the FCA. Husbands, after thirty years of marriage, never recognize anything positive about these natural qualities - so she should find someone who does.

They say a woman marries a man thinking she will be able to change him, while a man is afraid the woman he marries will change. Of course, his attitude is purely physical; he wants her to retain the same body and face he married. That's why FCAs must seek pleasure elsewhere - in the arms of a younger lover.

There are clubs and organizations whose purpose is to provide a place where FCAs and young men can meet, dance, and talk. There should be more of these. Besides providing a place for the like-minded to meet, they also serve as support groups where those involved can discuss situations and problems that may arise. The wonderful advantage to these places is the understanding that no one frequents them looking for marriage. With that kind of pressure eliminated, relationships are considerably more honest and upfront. Love is much freer to develop and be expressed for the same reason.

My message to all young men is to seek relationships with FCAs. Look for an age difference of twenty to thirty years because a larger difference can often be more exciting and rewarding for both parties. I personally prefer postmenopausal woman, but that's a subjective opinion. They have powerful but often sleeping libidos, and they certainly have no reason to be interested in older men as society would like them to. In fact, they may even have older men at home, holding down their recliners while their women are in your arms. We'll talk about how to catch one in a later chapter.

When an FCA is in the throes of multiple orgasms, her upper lip curls tight over her teeth and her eyes narrow to unseeing slits of ecstasy, those fine wrinkles at the corners of the eyes and along the lip line become tremendously erotic. They indicate a sensual ripeness that young girls simply cannot attain. A fact of nature that cannot be denied is that a woman remains sexual for her whole life, while a man runs out of steam by his seventies or eighties. The problem for the woman is how and where to find partners. I personally know three women over ninety years of age who are still sexually active (though one passed away while I have been working on this book). The other two are active to this day. How do I know this? One woman, a dear friend, has been open to discussing the subject with me. She has partners, one at a time, while the second woman's lover is a good friend of mine. She has money to lavish gifts on her lover, and the one who passed away let me know several times that she was available and ready whenever I was; she even physically groped me at a crowded party.

These women, and many more who I don't know about because they are much too discreet, don't seek men their own age for obvious reasons. They require partners considerably younger. So I say, why not start earlier, like fifties or sixties?

Of course this appreciation comes with experience—a form of conditioned reflex one might suggest.

"The older the violin, the sweeter the music."

"Les vieilles casseroles font les meilleurs potages." "Wine improves with age."

Need I go on?

Chapter 3

Selkirk (Pulaski) 1948

In the late forties, my buddies and I were too young to have real summer jobs. We were satisfied with mowing lawns in summer and shoveling driveways in winter for our spending money. But that meant that we had plenty of spare time to take off on our bikes, go to the old swimming hole, build huts in the woods, fly the model planes we had built during the winter, play sandlot softball—a kid's life was wonderful in those days. No TV, no electronic games, no phone in your pocket, only the fifteen-minute radio shows before dinner and *Gang Busters* on Friday night, *BigLittle* books and comic books to read, and an occasional "eight-pager." Yes, life was great—*as long as we were home by dinner time*. That was imperative. The family sat around the table for dinner every evening without fail. And we ate what was put before us.

Many people owned what we called *camps*, usually on lakes or ponds, primarily used on weekends for camping, fishing, swimming, boating, or just relaxing. A camp was a simple wood frame house, unfinished stud walls on the inside—walls that often didn't reach the roof structure—with a basic kitchen, bathroom, and closets, with or without electricity. Very simple, the camps were unheated except for a woodstove or fireplace.

This was rustic, leisure living—up and out in the morning, perhaps a card game at night. Even the kids knew card games back then. The family of one of my playmates, Lenny, had such a camp at Selkirk, New York, where the Salmon River empties into Lake Ontario. Local friends owned a boat rental and bait business, the running of which was usually left to their two teenage boys. The younger of the two, Jackson, was our age. It was not unusual for us kids to be left there alone for a number of days if the parents had to return home for some reason. On one such occasion, Jackson, Lenny, Ed, and I had a very exciting, educational experience.

It was the end of summer. Children would be returning to school the following week. The shoreline of Lake Ontario north of Selkirk was lined with one cabin after the other. They were mostly empty, closed up for the season. Jackson, Lenny, Ed, and I decided to walk up the sandy beach at sunset, joshing, talking, and skipping the occasional stone across the lake.

When we saw lights on in one of the camps, Jackson said, the owner was an old maid schoolteacher from Oswego. We could see two FCAs, playing cards and drinking what we assumed to be alcohol and coffee. The window shades were not pulled down all the way because no one was left in the area. It was probably their last night of vacation. It had become too dark for them to see us about thirty feet away on the beach, but because their lights were on, we could see them. When one got up to replenish the drinks, she leaned down and instigated a bit of kissing and fondling. Oh boy! This looked really interesting, but how much longer were they going to just play cards. We assumed that they would quit, undress, and go to bed, so a glimpse of them naked was about all we could expect.

Were we willing to wait it out? Seeing them kissing and drinking didn't really ring a bell with us. Remember, we were just kids. But we sure sensed something big—and we were very eager to learn.

So we stood around on the beach, shuffling along up and back crunching seashells underfoot. We could easily keep track of what they were doing and didn't want to miss anything, assuming that it would only be a few-minute show of mature nudity at best. How long does it take ladies to get ready for bed anyway?

Suddenly, and without warning, the clothes came off and the lovemaking began — right there before our eyes. The house was built on blocks, low to the ground. The porch, only a foot off the sand, surrounded the house on the front and right side. There were two windows, one on the front next to the front door and one on the right side. Below the window on the front wall was a daybed — the playing field as it were.

We were able to crawl up to the windows on our hands and knees and find ourselves twenty-four inches from the action. We could see it all, almost smell it. We would quietly change windows, two to a window. No dildos appeared, which didn't register with me at the time, but it does now when I think back on it. I guess battery-operated sex aids came much later. But I think these ladies performed quite well without them. It was all hands and mouths, pussy from above, pussy from below, mutual masturbation, sixty- nine, kissing, sucking, licking, moaning, groaning, gasping, crying, whimpering. It was *un*believable.

Actually, it was a very beautiful, erotic sight that only women together can perform.

Lenny at one point began whispering, "C'mon. Let's go."

We responded, "Lenny, you're nuts. This is too good — a once-in-a-lifetime chance."

"Aw, c'mon. It's late, and —"

Then Ed asked, "Lenny, did you jerk off? You did, didn't you? That's why you're ready to leave."

Lenny put his head down and sheepishly admitted, "Yeah." Ah…memories.

Chapter 4

How To

So how does a relationship between an FCA and a younger man begin? It can't really be initiated by the older woman, or society calls her a predator. The same applies to today's cougars; an unfortunate category of today's women who make no bones about what they want out of life. Mrs. Robinson of *The Graduate* fame, falls into that category. There is no challenge to seducing a woman who wants to be seduced anyway. No, the desirable women I'm interested in are *not* the obvious willing ones. I'm talking about the seemingly unapproachable ones who are, in fact, smoldering and vulnerable; but even they don't realize it or admit it— even to themselves. Everyone fantasizes, though it is seldom admitted and never discussed, similar to masturbation. An older woman—heaven forbid that she should admit to fantasizing about some young man twenty years her junior and then satisfying herself. Of course, we joke about the "pool guy" or the UPS deliveryman, but even that is a tiny inkling of what *really* goes on in older women's fantasy world. It's what stokes their fire. All those bodice- ripper novels are written *by* women *for* women because those writers know how to push the right buttons that get the right results.

A young man must realize that seducing an FCA takes time—sometimes a long time. Young girls today jump into bed on the first or second date. Girls in their late twenties and thirties may take a couple of dates longer. But remember, they are desperate by this age, looking for Mr. Right. My FCAs are never desperate because they are not looking for a husband; in fact, they are not even looking to have an affair even though they are ripe for one — but certainly not with a much younger man. They must be seduced slowly, while they are not aware of the young man slithering around them like a snake in the dark until the FCA wakes up one day thinking, *OMG, I have* feelings for him. Actually, if the young man is adept, the FCA will develop feelings for him during the process, much to her surprise. And the subject of marriage is never discussed. If it does come up, it is always the young man who suggests it, never the FCA.

I myself experienced a situation with a French FCA, who I had known for twelve years and liked very much as a friend. I never suggested anything more, never made a move because I knew that she was averse to more than a friendly relationship. She was satisfied with her life and her job. Her grown children were established and doing well. We were close enough, though our relationship was purely professional, that I said, upon return from a business trip to Brazil, "Let's have lunch next week."

It was vacation time in France, so many neighborhood restaurants were closed. I picked her up from the photo lab where she worked, and she asked, "Do you know of a restaurant in the *quartier* that is open this month?"

When I answered that yes, I thought I did know of a couple, she turned to me and said, "We are adults; turn left at the next corner. I've prepared *le déjeuner* at home."

She and her husband had been involved in the French Resistance during World War II and the occupation of Paris by the Germans. They were very active; she ran messages among the members, and was, in fact, held several times by the Gestapo. When we were together in Paris, she would point out places where she would deposit or pick up messages. They divorced soon after the war ended, due to the stress of the war on the marriage and his need to continue the excitement of illicit activities.

She had two grown children from that marriage and shied away from any man who approached her or showed interest in her.

She was certainly attractive, but during the years I knew her, I never made any move, other than to be always courteous, always correct, and always make her smile. Apparently she sensed something happening between us, which, though never to my knowledge expressed by me, was true. She really did not want to enter into any relationship and was not looking for an affair of any kind, but *voila*, she awakened one day and realized that, in fact, she was in love with me — a man thirteen years her junior. This fact she learned from my passport, which I had left on her mantle upon return from London, and was never of concern to me. I was certainly not expecting that and explained to her that I intended to leave France and move to Brazil so I was not apt for beginning an affair. She assured me that she would help me in any way she could and wouldn't do anything to hinder me from leaving Paris. No scenes or hysterics or the like would ensue. So we began a sweet, full-on relationship — no holds barred. She was a marvelous cook, as are most French women.

Postmenopausal women are sexually torrid but so often neglected. She ended up in the hospital. Her doctor guessed, by the look in her eyes and the lilt in her attitude, just what had happened. And he was correct. The ideal FCAs are often, if not usually, postmenopausal, but it seems our affair reignited her female plumbing, which churned back into action, resulting in sudden hemorrhaging and a couple of days in the hospital. The doctor, who had known her for years, chuckled and congratulated her — and gave me a wink and a nod. The problem was quickly resolved.

First, you must realize that, in the heart and soul of every FCA, a little pig is sleeping — yes, I said a little *pig* is sleeping.

A woman can go through life without that naughty little pig ever being prodded awake. And many of them do, because it requires the right partner to rouse that little pig and tease it out of hiding, and unfortunately, it is seldom the husband who recognizes the potential and accomplishes the awakening. When it is aroused in an FCA, it becomes a recognizable trait, readily visible to a man of experience who has the necessary talent to awaken her. When he gazes into the eyes of an FCA even from across the room, those little pig eyes are gazing back at him. She would be appalled if he suspected her fantasies.

She could never express them in words or dare ask a man to help her realize them. It is up to an experienced partner to lead her to them and *through* them. There is no doubt that "a woman well f- - - -d is a woman in love." As a female friend once answered to my question, "Do you think sex is dirty?" "If it's well done it is" she responded. She was French of course.

I have asked many women what part of the body they consider the most important where sex is concerned. Most immediately settle on the brain because — well, you can imagine the intellectual answers I get. "Because we reason with our brain, blah, blah," or "The brain controls our subconscious, which in turn, blah, blah."I see the brain as our human version of a computer's hard drive, primarily for memory storage. But we're working with *the moving parts* here in this exercise.

So my response is simply this: The mouth is the most dominant organ with regard to sexual actions, and I can illustrate my point in several easy steps.

Step 1. The groundwork. We meet someone somewhere, maybe at a conference.

"Hello, my name is Jules. And yours?"

"My name is Mady. Pleased to meet you, Jules." (First to act, the mouth.)

He seems like a nice guy, and he is good-looking. (More talking.)

She seems intelligent, and she's crazy cute. (More talking)

I'd like to see him again. (More talking)

They decide to get together for coffee one day soon. It goes well. (More talking)

They meet for dinner. More talking plus a peck on the cheek. (Only the mouth is in play)

Dinner again. More talking and then more kissing.

Step 2. The kiss.

Serious kissing now. Would you like to come up for a drink?

Serious kissing, sucking sounds. (Poor dick is a bystander but standing tall by now, I'm sure.) They move from the couch to the bedroom.

Now the mouth is making its way down, down, first to the breasts and then to *nirvana.*

Step 3. Orgasm one.

The mouth finds nirvana. (First three steps are completed with *only the mouth* in the title role.)

Step 4. Orgasm two.

Finally dick gets his chance to enter the fray. ("It's about time.")

Step 5. Orgasm three (or more).

The mouth bats cleanup of the musky elixir — my *satori.*

"Lay back, my love. Relax …relax. But leave me access."

So we see how the mouth is the dominant organ from first word to final taste? As tension mounts, both parties are frantic because they each want their mouths to be everywhere at once on the partner's body — up here, down there, over there. And c'mon, you know what I mean. Of course other parts are working feverishly in the background, trying to keep up—the eyes, the hands. Actually any number of other moving parts certainly contribute, but the mouth is the clear winner. *N'est-ce pas?*

So these *un*-awakened women will swear up and down that:

1. they are not interested in an affair and
2. certainly not with a younger man, and
3. sex is not important anymore anyway. That's in the past anyway.....and at *my* age?

They must be approached stealthily and with great subtleness. They must *never* suspect they are being considered for seduction. They cannot be approached with brusqueness but, rather, with *courtoisie* and finesse. If they suspect for a moment that a young man is trying to approach them romantically, they are *obliged* to immediately become defensive—to resist any recognized advance, invitation, or suggestion that there is interest on their part even though it produces a slight tickle of flattery. It is imbedded in their psyche. They must not be faced with the option to say, *yes* or *no*, because it will always be—in fact it *must* be – *no*.

> Maybe we could have dinner sometime? *No.* Meet for a drink? *No.*
> "I could never be attracted to a younger man."
> "Imagine …Why he could be my son."
> "No, *no*, I would look *ridiculous*—no, never, *not me.*

Women of a certain age are very fragile, uncertain of their attractiveness, convinced that no one would be interested in them anyway, and will tell the world, "I'm certainly not interested in getting involved with anyone at my age."

We'll see about that.

First-year anatomy students learn about the human body by dissecting corpses; mechanics learn about motors by taking them apart. But that is not how men learn about women. (It has been tried, but not successfully). Understanding women is a long process, much like carefully making your way through a minefield; any wrong step can mean danger — either a mishap, which might be mended, or the end of what might have been a beautiful friendship. Many men never achieve a working level of understanding women. We observe them every day; just look in your daily newspaper. As of this writing, politicians, actors, and men with power over subordinate women in business seem to be the worst offenders. FCA's must be approached with courtesy, tenderness, and *finesse*.

It's been years since the FCA was courted or remembered how to act coy. She probably was married, or may still be married. She may have raised a couple of children and may have known only one man intimately in her life. Self-confidence in dating skills was perhaps awkward even as a young girl. Marriage happened, as it so often does to young women who often are not ready. We see the result all around us. Check out your friends, and you will see what I mean.

By the time they reach FCA age, these women have an internal dissatisfaction with life, without really realizing why. They know something is missing; they just can't define it or discuss it. They are not abused; they are simply *neglected*.

Ask your average doctor; he or she hears it all the time. "Doctor, I don't know what's wrong with me. I just don't feel well. My husband isn't interested in me anymore. I'm overweight. We don't go out nights anymore like we used to." And so on and so on.

The doctor, who sees these cases every day, prescribes a sugar pill or maybe an antidepressant and sends her on her way. The doctor knows what she needs, but he can't prescribe it. You, young man, will become the provider of that which is missing — tenderness, attention, companionship, and understanding ... and more. That becomes your responsibility.

My definition of an FCA is an attractive woman (notice I didn't say beautiful or even pretty), who would never *think* of entering into a relationship with a man "young enough to be my *son*."

That is a tremendous psychological hurdle, which can never be surmounted. So a young man should never try to *jump* that hurdle; he'll lose, because he is forcing the issue. Go *around it*. Instead of her saying, "I could never go to bed with that young man," the intention is to have her wake up one morning in bed with the young man, completely satisfied and radiant, saying, "My God, how did *that* happen?"

Now if she is in her late forties, fifties, or sixties, she's only supposed to see older men? So you think a guy in his sixties or more is going to stimulate her into doing something naughty and exciting? I think not.

Find ways to be where women are in casual groups with friends and common interests. Your presence will not be threatening to them. Be friendly, at ease, courteous, and attentive; and, above all, make them laugh and pay attention to them. Remember, women are sensitive to the little things — the small gestures and the small remarks; subtle compliments about little things such as their hair, their dress, and even the way they walk. But this must not be delivered in a too personal intimation. It is called, *complicity*, and it is very important that it be created between the parties. The little subtle glances between partners and being in near proximity without acknowledging one another, specifically if a husband is around, can add tension and excitement to the situation. Tension is an active part of excitement. But be careful. I have seen a five-year-old girl recognize romance in the air when an older woman was in the beginnings of a love interest.

Above all, never ask an FCA her age. Her age is irrelevant; if you find her attractive, she is attractive — *because of her age*, not in spite of it. I have been involved with much older women for years without ever knowing or caring about their ages. It may come out eventually in conversation or by simply doing the math over things that have been said, but ignore age and allow it to add fuel to the excitement of the relationship.

When a woman is self-critical, be quick to counter that remark with a complimentary comeback. Listen to what she is saying. Add to it when you can. FCA's will say, "What subjects of conversation could I possibly have with a young man?" That comment in itself shows a defensive attitude — a mental barrier that must be worn away gradually. Doing it is a challenge for the young man, but each chip that falls without her realizing is a positive step. Each step of the way, she must become comfortable with the changing relationship before a further step can be taken. She must never feel that she was jostled awake as to what was happening, and she must never be put in a situation requiring a *yes* or *no* reaction.

This is easy in an equal-age scenario, because the woman or girl is expecting the man to make certain moves and deciding how she will respond, but we are not dealing with an equal-age scenario. In our scenario, the FCA must not sense that she is falling ever so slowly into a more serious relationship than she expected or even thinks she could accept because then she begins to *think* about it — and that is to be avoided. Rather, she should look forward to a next encounter simply because the last time was enjoyable; non- committal; and, of course, *harmless*.

When I was nineteen and a university student, I met forty-nine-year-old Mary, a vivacious, widowed FCA living in Boston. I met her married daughter, who was just two years older than I, her son-in-law; and her two (eventually three) grandchildren. We became friends, a social foursome in fact. It took a while, but she and I just naturally became lovers — totally unbeknownst to her daughter (who would have been surprised, mortified and probably even furious at her mother) and son-in-law (who would probably have said to me, "way to go, man"). She claimed that she didn't understand how it all had happened, but I knew *exactly* how it had happened, and she did too, really. But she was never put in a position where she was forced to make a *yes* or *no* decision at every step throughout the long seduction. She came to New York after a six-year affair, to see me sail for France on the *Queen Mary*.

She was naive in many ways, having married early while lacking real life experience — except for an on-going, less successful affair with a married man she had dated many years ago in her student days and who lived in Canada. He only visited from time to time and, apparently, being her age, was an old-school lover of the worst kind. One Sunday, after attending Trinity Episcopal Church in Copley Square, Boston, we stopped in at the home of Peter, an acquaintance of hers who I recognized immediately as being gay. (She recognized nothing at all, as innocent older women were prone to do in those days.) The dry martinis began to flow abundantly, and dear Peter began to come on to me — a nineteen-year-old guy with a forty- nine-year-old FCA. I'm certain he must have thought that, of course I was gay also. By that time, we were all high as kites; he was trying to put his hands down my pants without Mary seeing. I was defending myself discreetly because I knew Mary had no idea what was going on, being three sheets to the wind anyway, and I didn't want to make a scene over her friend's behavior. When we finally extricated ourselves from the situation and were walking to Mary's Marlboro Street apartment(where we finished what we had started at Peter's), I explained what had been going on with Peter. She had absolutely no idea that he was gay or that he was all over me. I also don't believe that Peter had any idea of what was going on between Mary and me. Who would? Peter kept insisting that he and I play squash together one day.

That never happened.

Patience and stealth was always my method. Had someone suggested such an outcome when we first met, she would have been insulted and furious because the very idea would represent a serious flaw in her character. Her daughter (about my age) never suggested, "Mom, I think he has designs on you." But other older women with a flair for sexual intrigue would have sensed and understood. Those women, call it intuition, I guess, always seem to possess a sixth sense about such things — maybe because of their own inner frustrations. Mary herself could no longer use the age-old "I could *never* do such a thing" defense, because she had, in fact, *done* such a thing. However, once she got a taste of it, there was no turning back. She simply accepted it— maybe even coyly admitting the affair to very close lady friends but certainly not to her daughter. Our relationship lasted for six years until I finished my studies at MIT and left the country, which was the logical way for it to end. I heard through her grandson that she eventually married the wealthy widower husband of her best girlfriend—a man considerably older but who provided security for the rest of her days. She remained attractive till the end.

It takes patience, but doesn't that make the challenge and the quest more interesting and exciting and the result more fulfilling?

You bet it does.

The younger man will be rewarded for his sticktoitiveness.

Chapter 5

The Bidet

A subject that must be considered before we go much further concerns personal hygiene. America—the land of plenty, the land of the million-dollar bathrooms, with their sunken showers; gyrating whirlpool tubs large enough for the entire family; gold-plated fixtures with multiple throbbing, pulsating, massaging showerheads; carpeted floors …But wait!

Where's the bidet?

Oh, you mean that funny thing the Europeans have in their *salles de bains* that Americans find so, well, embarrassing, actually? Apparently those little old American ladies in tennybumpers (my term for the practical footwear worn by the elderly on organized vacation travel) give little thought to—*washing their butts.*

As the French bellhop replied when the American dowager asked, "Is that to wash the baby in?"

"No Madame. That is to wash the baby *out* in."

That is certainly *part* of the story. But I do not understand why, for decades, Americans have delighted in deriding one of the most essential accessories to personal intimate cleanliness. Americans think they are the cleanest people on earth? "Don't we wash our hands after going to the bathroom?" (No. Studies show that actually, they don't.) But what about the millions of dollars Americans spend on bathrooms and beauty products? Doesn't that prove anything? No. Actually it proves only that money is not the problem. Studies have shown that American women tend to only wash their hands *if there are other women present in the ladies' room*. If not, out they go; and what a mess they leave behind. (It's my lady friends who tell me this.)

Sales of high-priced beauty products are greater in the United States than in any other country. Many of these products *wouldn't need a market* if we had bidets in our homes. Those products that deal with odors, burning and itching, and yeasts deal with problems created mainly by poor personal hygiene; it's as simple as that.

Yeast belongs in the bread, and vinegar belongs in the salad. We are a nation of dirty bottoms, and that is unfortunate and rather disgusting.

Women shave under their arms; shave their legs; and use underarm deodorants, expensive creams, lotions, potions, and perfumes at thirty plus dollars an ounce.

But they have dirty bottoms!

The same goes for our men. Men use underarm deodorants, expensive aftershaves, and colognes but often have skid marks in their shorts. I was told by a woman that she began to suspect her husband of having an affair "when he stopped soiling his underwear." He *was*, in fact, having an affair. She was right.

Adoption of the bidet in this nation of dirty bottoms would upset the personal products market—a market peddling goop and sprays designed to cover up that which regular use of a bidet, soap, and warm water probably could have avoided in the first place.

A trip down the supermarket aisle marked "Feminine Needs" is revealing— Summer's Eve, Feminique, Femme Fresh. Or how about Vagisil, *for feminine itching*; Monistat 7, *more than just a cure*; and Gyne-Lotrimin? If I had those kinds of problems, I would call my plumber to install a bidet, *stat*! The visual image of a woman wielding a ten-ounce spray can of Femme Fresh, turned upside down between her legs, would be comical if it weren't so serious. Come to think of it, spray cans don't work upside down; that image becomes even funnier.

And since we're on the subject; why the discrimination against men? Where is the "Masculine Needs" section? Or maybe we should just label the beer cooler *Masculine Needs*.

And another thing, ladies. Men are pigs; we all know that. They are too lazy to lift the seat when they pee if they think they will not be caught. So I have a better idea. Ladies, if the seats were always *up*, men couldn't pee on them. Wouldn't it be better if toilet seats were spring-loaded so they would *always* be up and clean until *you* put them down to sit? An ultraviolet light could be installed to sterilize the seat when in the upright position. Don't forget. Liberal society is dictating that *anything goes* gender-wise. Even kids can choose what they think they want to be.

In France there is no problem. I went to the 24 Hours of Le Mans car race with Ed, an American friend who had just arrived. When we needed to relieve ourselves, we entered a long tent with urinals left and right. We stepped up to go when Ed realized that women were walking right behind him on their way to toilets in the back. He was so shocked he peed on himself; trying to stop the stream, he subsequently dropped the expensive race program he had just purchased into the urinal. Public urination is not a crime in France. Stop the car, get out, turn your back, and go — so civilized and so natural.

The very existence of all those products mentioned above goes a long way toward proving my point. When I lived in countries where every home, hotel bathroom, and even many public bathrooms had bidets, I never encountered women suffering from these things that seem to afflict the American dirty bottoms. As I said before, yeast belongs in the bread and the cheese....Well, you get the gist.

"But we Americans bathe daily," they say.

Well, some do; most don't. The bidet is used every time the toilet is used, every time clothing is changed, before going to bed, before sex, after sex, and so on. The tub or shower cannot be considered a replacement for the bidet.

The very thought of having a spontaneous sexual interlude with a partner who hasn't washed "it" since early morning or the night before (if then) and has been sitting on it and peeing through it throughout the workday. Ladies, your *happy place* should be ready for service any time of the day or night, *non*? During a quiet dinner, a nice bottle of wine, and some slow dancing, my mind starts to thinking — considering all it's been through (or has been through it), *hmmm*? It may do for a *quickie*, but it certainly stifles *good* sex. And forget those feminine sprays and silly little *towlettes* you carry in your purse.

By the time American children are five years old, they have been taught to believe that their genitals are dirty — something to be ashamed of. And considering the way they are raised, that is true. They mustn't be looked at, explored, touched, played with, or shown to anyone. As the child grows, the repression about the body continues. They realize that their genitals urinate, defecate, menstruate, and ejaculate and that bad odors can emanate from there. When a young girl starts her menses, it is not a pleasant experience for her.

Part of her education should have been about the importance of a bidet; a bath a day just won't do. I remember several unfortunate situations during my high school years in America, because girls didn't seem to have either the means or the smarts on how to take care of themselves — and the neighborhood dogs sensed it from far away. At Syracuse University fraternity row, one fraternity had a very large dog. The brothers would sit on the porch in summer and watch the dog stick his nose in the crotch of the guilty girls walking by.

Then all of a sudden, those same genitals, the source of so much shame and repression, become the very core of their sexual awakenings. The girls have certainly suffered much more than the boys in this respect. For the boys, it's been playtime for Peter (go blind or not) for a long time. Now the world begins to revolve around their "naughty parts," fueled by an overabundance of hormones.

Doctors I have questioned on the subject agree that many personal problems, such as hemorrhoids, yeast infections, and feminine itching and burning, could often be relieved or avoided altogether through improved personal hygiene.

American bathrooms are enormous by European standards, with plenty of room for bidet installations. Unfortunately, they are seldom requested of builders by homebuyers. Europeans have portables and swing-away models — any solution to accommodate a bidet in a small space. You may have to fill it from the sink, or it may be a plumber's tour de force, which swings away under the sink on wheels. But *mon dieu*, they'll never be without one. You may have to go down the hall for the toilet, but a bidet will always be at hand. American homebuilders sometimes install them in model homes in the high- dollar price range (to justify some of that otherwise wasted space, I guess). But the buyer uses them mostly as a conversation piece or to wash feet in. They think it gives a sophisticated, continental look to their new, overpriced home. I have had guests in my home mistake the bidet for a toilet and then get sprayed in the face when leaning over to flush it.

I love it when that happens!

I was never a part of the sixties hippie sexual revolution. Nor did I have any empathy with the straggle-haired American great unwashed as they came slogging through Europe following the hashish trail to Katmandu on their quest for pot and STDs and who knows what else. I could not, in my wildest nightmares, ever imagine touching one of those unkempt, slovenly flower children, yet they seemed to think they invented sex. But what *quality* of sex could they possibly have had considering the odoriferousness of their personal atmosphere? Maybe that's why the dope, alcohol, and incense sticks were so necessary.

The bidet's role in sex cannot be underestimated. Let's face it; oral sex is about as good as it gets. But without a bidet around, well, it kind of makes one think twice, doesn't it?

Why so much emphasis on cleanliness? The real subject of this book is the promotion of those wonderful, exciting FCAs and the young men who should discover and desire them.

The following chapters will cover subjects, relationships, and techniques that depend for their success on complete and total cleanliness for both partners.

Your mother told you to wear clean underwear in case you have an accident and are taken to a hospital. Believe me, there are much more important reasons for impeccable personal hygiene than that.

At work, on the street, in restaurants and bars, and at home—the dirty bottoms are everywhere.

Avoid them or convert them!

Louanges a Trois, 1996

Ils viennent au près de moi
pleins de joie et tendresse.
Avec l'espoir de cueillir
un câlin, une caresse.

Ils m'acceptent comme je suis,
sans me juger, *jamais*.
Pas comme les autres;
ceux qui simulent les baisers.

Leur présence seule suffit
à éloigner l'ennui.
Ils sont tout simplement
les joies de ma vie.

Ce sont ma femme et mes chiens.
Ils m'aiment; je les adore.
Faire un choix? Mais comment?
Ils valent plus que de l'or!

Car mes chiens sont mes gosses
en manteaux de fourrures,
et ma femme *"a du chien"*.
Que puis-je avoir de mieux?

Praises by Three

They come close to me,
full of joy and tenderness,
With the hope of receiving
just a hug, a caress.

They accept me as I am,
not ever judgmental.
Not like some others,
who would feign their embrace.

Their presence suffices
to drive away tedium.
They are, quite simply,
the joys of my life.

For my wife and my dogs
love me; I adore them.
Make a choice? How could I?
They're worth more than gold!

My dogs are my kids
dressed up in fur coats,
and my wife has *that something*
For what more could I hope?

Chapter 6

The Phases of Life

My years of experience and observation have led me to recommend a life plan based *not* on what society thinks but on what nature and the human body (plus the hormones) think. My own mother might well be shocked at my ideas, as she was in just the kind of somewhat repressive society I managed to sidestep.

Remember when one was expected to be engaged by the time a university decided that enough of your money had been collected? You had purchased a sufficient number of books that would eventually gather dust in a closet, so they gave you a nice certificate "suitable for framing," and the wedding took place in June? The happy couple went off into the sunset—he with a good entry-level job and she ready to produce and raise a family, join the PTA and bridge club and do the things expected of newlyweds. Live happily ever after? Till death do us part?

Well, not exactly.

After producing a couple of children (the easy part), many divorced and then married again—sometimes three times, maybe even more. I used to say I didn't make the same mistake *once*. It wasn't that I'm against marriage. I finally did it myself. And now, happily ever after and till death do us part both apply to me.

But first, I lived the life I'm promoting to you now.

My life has not been just one long hedonistic experience. It turned out to be a meaningful research program around the world, with emphasis on European women.

I am not an MD. Nor am I a psychologist or sexologist with diplomas from universities (other than MIT) on my wall. Every time I read sex studies (*The Hite Report* or Masters and Johnson or *Playboy*, for that matter), I sense that many people who respond anonymously to questionnaires are having their first go at creative writing. It's kind of vicarious fun to put your fantasies down on paper when you know no one is watching, with hopes of seeing them in print. However, I'm certain I have had firsthand experience that they can only dream about. My comments are based on my personal experiences and observations.

I love women. I adore women. My aim in life has always been to please women. They excite me, intrigue me, fascinate me, frustrate me, and aggravate me. But then, most men will tell you the same thing. Historically, women have always made the world turn. I have learned from women that I am capable of stimulating great emotions in them, but most men will tell you that also.

From the time I was born, I realized something — something quite marvelous in fact. I was physically and intellectually attracted to older women — *much* older women. I preferred their conversations, their looks, and their very presence. I found adult conversations more interesting, and I felt a strong physical/sexual attraction to some of those women that I never felt toward girls my own age. This seemed to be true whether I was ten, twenty, or thirty years old. The women I found attractive were always twenty or thirty years older. These feelings were intense and from the heart. The first love of my life was unbearably intense for over twenty-five years, in spite of the twenty-eight-year age difference.

Unnatural? I certainly don't think so. Why should I be considered unique in feeling such things? On the contrary, I believe most young men would love to spend a few years of their lives with the right FCA, but they don't have the savoir faire to do it. Who, male or female, never lusted for an older teacher? How I wished one would invite me to come to her house to "rake leaves" some day after school. *Oh, yeah!* And the freshman year, old maid teacher who didn't wear a bra under her blouse and slip or the sophomore year old maid social studies teacher who would lean her crotch into the corner of her desk when talking — those old gals were not kidding me. Their innocent minds were just as busy fighting subconscious fantasies as we were, but we didn't have the courage to offer our services; all we could do was joke among ourselves. "Boy, how I would like to Miss So-and-So." (Fill in the blank.)

Back in those days, *unmarried* was a requirement for grade school. But World War II changed all that. Young teachers could earn more working jobs for the war effort, and young soldiers wanted to marry before shipping off to war, so many older teachers were called back from retirement to teach.

Schoolteachers are certainly subjects for many teen sexual fantasies, but the social situation, laws, punishments, and danger of discovery are too strong.

Fantasies are strongest if left forever as fantasies. Once acted out, details enter in that destroy the perfect quality of a fantasy, reducing it to nothing more than *reality*. The romance is gone.

I followed my heart and my body, doing what felt natural to me. My partners simply did the same.

There are three phases to life — the young formative years, the middle productive years, and the later restive or coasting years.

During the formative years, we achieve our education, which includes upbringing, manners, school, and university, and, of course, discover sex.

During the productive years, we work at a profession, have children, and continue the same old sex.

During the restive years, we begin to relax, lie back a little, and think about sex once in a while.

Notice I didn't *qualify* the sex yet because it is different for each person in all three phases.

The first phase is also when sex education takes place because it includes puberty and beyond. This is when young men should seek FCAs and spend ten or fifteen years in their company. Fathers should urge their sons to avoid Susy Cream Cheese's giggly innocence and baby fat, but perhaps consider her mother or grandmother instead. Even if little Suzy is already the high school bicycle, she really has nothing much to offer. If she's fifteen, her mother is probably thirty-four — too young to qualify as a certified FCA. So grandmother might be in her early fifties - *ooooh*, the ideal age for a sexual meltdown.

He may not be quite ready for that for his first FCA, but she should be at least forty years old.

The thirties for a woman are about as unattractive as the teen years. They are confused about aging; the children are growing away from them; and they can't deal with the husband's disinterest, his slothful ways, or his love affair with the TV remote. They tend to be basket cases — not something our young men should be considering. If they have a "career," they can be even worse. They are so busy being aggressive business "persons" by day that it would take a trainer with chair and whip to tame them at night. They have no time to play and can't turn it off at night, slip into something "comfortable," and coax Clyde off the remote control. They have problems of their own that we don't need.

I'm not here to put down the thirty-year-old, but I do feel that they make lousy FCAs. Let's just agree that she is not yet ripe for our young men, *and she may never be.* It's up to her. While Stendhal's Julien and Sra. De Rênal were only eleven years apart, her thirty years during the nineteenth century would be comparable to well over forty years in our time. It's all about *attitude* of course.

I'm not the first to feel that a woman doesn't become interesting until the age of forty. Honoré de Balzac's Mme. Hanska, Stendhal's Sra. De Rênal, and even Thomas Jefferson, I believe expressed those sentiments at one time or another. The French accept younger-men-older-woman relationships more easily — with a wink, referring to them sometimes as "*Balzacian* affairs. "France, at this very moment while I am writing, has a president, Emmanuel Macron, who, as a teenager, fell in love with Brigitte, the drama coach at his high school, twenty-four years his senior. With that I can sympathize; in fact, I sent them a draft of this book and received confirmation of its arrival from his *chef du cabinet*.

But wait. There's more. They married in 2007. It took him a while to convince her, but he knew what he wanted and went for it. It may not happen often; the parents usually stifle such romances, which Macron's did by sending him away to school for several years, blaming the older woman where no blame is due. I'm proud of him and of Brigitte for ignoring other people's judgment. "It is my life, and that is it," he says and rightly so. Smart parents don't go ballistic when they learn that their seventeen-year-old son is having an affair with their good friend or maybe even their good friend's mother or wife. They just give it a wink and a nod.

I find that attitude extremely civilized and healthy. I was sorely disappointed by the outcome of the movie *The Graduate*. I was all for the affair with Mrs. Robinson, though I thought it took Benjamin much too long to get with the game. While watching the movie, I wanted to call out advice to Benjamin: *Go for it! Make the phone call! Forget plastics! Shag Mrs. Robinson!* But it was obvious. The doofus had no idea what he was doing or how to go about it. He was a typical American immature innocent. He should have devoted several years to Mrs. Robinson and never taken up with the spoiled daughter, Elaine — a romance obviously headed for disaster. But Hollywood and the censors could have it no other way.

I lived a similar episode with the mother of a boyhood pal while he was stationed in Europe. I would stop by their house and chat with her, while her husband was passed out upstairs in a drunken stupor. Beer was the drink of choice. She was straight out of Fellini — mature, heavy breasts and quickly wet to the touch. With about fifty years on the odometer, she was obviously very needy and, while a bit shopworn (three kids, and she drank too), still brought the sap to the surface, resulting in a memorable standing knee trembler with her back bent over the kitchen sink.

Memories are made of this.

Chapter 7

In the Beginning

From the day I was born, I was in love. I know that sounds crazy, but it's true. She was a close family friend, but she lived far, far away — so far away, in fact, that I only saw her every few years. Now what do you believe? Does absence make the heart grow fonder? Or is it out of sight, out of mind? I didn't make those up, but I've given them a lot of thought over the years. And they both have validity.

When the family drove the 1,200 miles to visit my grandparents and aunts, uncles aqnd cousins, my expectations were to see the object of my love, though at that age I had no influence over my family's travel plans. I just had to hope that *she* would be included during our visits. There were ralatives to see on both sides of the family, besides the grandparents, with their old-world sloppy kisses, and mini reunions here and there. I lived through all of that while longing for the occasions when *she* would be present. In those days, our family didn't express emotions in big physical ways — not a lot of hugging and kissing — so my feelings were frustrated and held inside, never discussed with anyone, neither friend nor family member. As you have probably surmised, *she* was considerably older than I — twenty-seven years older should be in fact. But my feelings never wavered. As I grew older, my longing increased, and being near her became quite painful, although visits were sometimes years apart. Of course, she knew nothing of this; she had a life, a husband, a son older than I, friends, activities, and the lot. During our infrequent visits and divided time together, any display of affection on my part would have seemed strange and out of place, while at the same time my insides were boiling with longing. I don't remember those feelings as being sexual but, rather, a desire to hold, hug, kiss, and stay close to her.

Our road trips out west were pure folklore. We nurtured our 1936 two-door Oldsmobile through World War II and more, until 1948, when a new postwar car became available. The Oldsmobile was not an *old* car. It was simply *our* car — a virtual tank, made of real steel, with a straight-eight, 100-hp motor and eight spark plugs sticking up the flat head, ready to stall the motor if driven too fast through big puddles.

I can see my father now, in the rain with the hood up, trying to dry those eight spark plugs with a handkerchief so the car would start and we could continue on.

We were two adults and two kids, plus a toy Boston terrier named Skippy in the back seat, the restless kids playing what has to be the stupidest game kids ever invented. "I looked at you last. ""No, I looked at you last." We were driving our parents to distraction and Skippy, meanwhile, was car-sick, so threw up at regular intervals.

Burma-Shave signs were like gold nuggets, sprinkled over the US highway system with words of wisdom for bored travelers. Our parents cooked up various games to occupy us, such as counting white horses or making license plate lists by states — anything to keep us from arguing in the back seat. "Mom, his feet are over on my side." "They are not." "They are too." "They are not." At which time my Mother's ultimate threat came forth: "If you kids don't stop, I'm going to knock your heads together till they fall off and roll on the floor." This brought forth gales of laughter from us kids. I believe Skippy even smiled - and then probably threw up again.

Back in those days, there were no freeways. When driving cross-country on two-lane roads, we had no choice but to search for those small route number signs nailed to telephone poles, while threading our way through the center of every city on our route. And the arguments—Dad driving while Mother navigated.

"I think we should have turned left back there." "Why didn't you tell me *back there?*"

"You're going too fast. I couldn't see the sign. I was cleaning up dog vomit."

And so on.

Father was a stickler for getting on the road before sunup and stopping at sundown. He was on the road a lot for his work and loved to eat where the truckers ate—where the fried foods were greasier but the homemade pies were the best. Mother was more concerned with clean bathrooms - "don't touch *anything* and for heaven's sake, *don't* sit on the toilet seat" - rather than the quality of the food. And of course finding places to eat was not that simple. There were no fast food chains. There were no motels. But tourist cabins were beginning to spring up; and we loved them. Each cabin had one room with bath and unfinished interior walls, but the car was parked alongside for easy access and an easy early start the next morning.

Our 1936, two-door Oldsmobile had very limited trunk space, just a hump on the back with two shelves inside, which also held the spare tire and tools. One trip that stands out in my memory was when my parents decided that we could save time and money if we could take food with us. We could reduce lost time searching for places to eat plus the cost of eating out. So Dad fastened a wooden box with small drain holes onto the back bumper that could hold a twenty-five-pound block of ice and *a cooked ham* for snacking at comfort stops and dinner time and even breakfast in a tourist cabin. *Yeah, man*—ham, ham, and more salty ham.

We were looking more and more like something from the *Grapes of Wrath*. Hungry? You're hungry? Here, eat some ham. Still hungry? Have some more ham. It didn't take long for us kids to whine, "Mom, I'm thirsty." "Mom, I'm dying. Ahghh ... water ...*please ...gotta have water*."

During wartime, the speed limit was 35 mph in order to save gas and rubber tires. So, 1,200 miles at 35 mph, and no freeways? That's two very long, boring days with two small kids and a dog, eating salty ham. *Try that*, you folks with your fancy motor homes with beds, a toilet, and a refrigerator cruising on smooth, wide divided highways. But then, you miss the rattlesnake farms, the two-headed calves, and the dinosaur bone attractions along the old state highways.

♫ *Route 66, where are you?* ♪

Howard Johnson came to the rescue in the early thirties – a recognizable orange roof over clean restrooms, twenty-eight flavors of ice cream, and edible food. The latter was maybe not as good as the greasy truck stops Dad preferred, but it was dependably okay according to Mom's criteria. And the restrooms were clean; let's not forget *that*. They were few and far between, but boy did that orange roof look good to us; and 28 flavors of ice cream.

When I was a little shaver, three cute girls stopped at our house to walk me to kindergarten every morning (which was right across the street from our house). My parents thought this was cute, particularly my father, who adored little girls, as men usually do. As luck would have it, one was blond, one had dark hair, and the third was a redhead. I only remember the name of the Irish redhead because the way she said her name was so adorable. Every single day my Father would ask her, "And what is your name?" just to hear her say all in one breath, "Patsypatriciajanebrady." Bless her heart, I wonder where PatsyPatriciaJaneBrady is today – if she still *is* today.

In 1936, when I was five years old and in kindergarten, I had my first chance at a stage career, dancing and singing. And I remember it all in great detail — even the melody of my song.

One day in class, the teacher asked if anyone knew how to tap dance. I held up my hand, though I had never tap-danced in my short life. I knew that you clacked your feet on the floor — *anybody* can do that — so, without even an audition, I got the job. The role consisted of little me performing the opening *and* the closing number of our big kindergarten stage production on parents' night. Both of those numbers required me to tap dance and sing. I had two songs to memorize, a white suit and tam-o'-shanter with a red pom-pom, a red foulard; and of course, tap shoes.

We lived across the street from School N° 27 in Albany, New York (all of the schools were numbered, no names). The night of the performance, Dad carried me across the street to the school to avoid any chance of me falling in some dirt, encountering a mud puddle, or somehow getting my spotless white suit dirty.

Following are the opening and the closing songs I sang solo, with piano accompaniment. Mother had saved the words, handwritten on an envelope, which I found in a box of the many things mothers think of to save for their children to eventually throw away years later. I remember everything about it all — even the melody — after eighty plus years.

*Clickity clack, clackity clack,*down to stage front, bow to the audience and start singing with the piano:

Opening Number

See us the kindergarten group,
All here to wish a welcome true.
We'll try to do our very best,
And hope you'll like us too.
Clickity clack, clickity clack

Finale

Now we must say good night,
To all our friends so dear.
And now our song is through
We hope you liked us too.
And so, thank you all.
For coming out to call
And let us say, in a nice way
Good night and farewell to all.

What a success for my theatrical debut. The applause was deafening; the audience was on its feet screaming approval (you know how parents can be.)

Well, maybe that was just Mom and Dad making all the noise — *sorry.*

So, it would seem that I was off to a good start with the ladies, at least in kindergarten. But it wasn't so, because there was one who was always on my mind but so very far away. In the meantime, I might have had feelings for several teachers in grade school but never for classmates my age.

One time, on a Friday night seventh grade hayride (hay rides in summer, sleigh rides in winter) I *sort* of kissed a girl, because others around me were doing it, and I remember not liking it at all. *Eeeeuw yucky!*

Throughout high school, I was not a nerd. I played basketball on my church team and for my high school; we were usually at least county champions. I was president of the National Honor Society, president of Hi-Y, and president of Key Club. I won the Bausch & Lomb Science Award. I was a good student but simply not interested in girls my age as something other than friends. The jocks got the cute girls of course, but it seems like everyone found a partner, went steady, broke up, found another, and so on. I simply wasn't interested. And in any case, my heart was over a thousand miles away.

I dated when it was an obligation, such as the Junior Prom or the Senior Ball. I really don't believe even the heavy daters were actually getting laid back in those days; even light petting was considered very daring and caused guilt feelings among my buddies who discussed their progress in such matters. I never even came close to that. It's funny; when I talk to people my age now about those days in high school, many of them assure me that more was going on than I knew about. That certainly could be true, though guys my age at the time loved to brag about *how far they got* with Mary, Rita, or Jean. I gathered that a hand inside the blouse was about it. Now, a hand inside the blouse of that freshman-year teacher? *Yeah, you bet!*

I saw no pregnancies in high school. If they were going all the way, they were being *really* careful.

When I turned sixteen, I got my driver's license and was able to work real jobs during summer vacation. That meant a shorter period of time to earn the limit allowed before my father would lose me as a dependent on his income taxes, more spending money for me to save for the upcoming year, and more free time remaining since I could no longer earn money.

I used that time to hitchhike to Kansas City to visit family and friends on my own. I still had one grandmother; aunts and uncles; and, of course, *the one* — who, upon my arrival, dropped her extra set of car keys in my hand. I became her chauffer, and I had the use of her car to visit relatives, to take my grandmother shopping and to dinner and a movie, and to put to other such uses. I, of course, became friends with her circle of friends — mostly wives of doctors with whom she played golf, visited, shopped, did volunteer work, and whatever else women do together. My feelings were still pent up within me; I never made a move or said a word. And that was okay; just being near was enough compared to the years of separation and suffering.

One evening, we were sitting on a double chaise longue on her veranda drinking Cokes and talking. She was on my right. The drinks were on a small table also on our right. Until that moment, there had been absolutely no physical contact of any kind — *ever*! But whenever we were in close proximity, the air seemed electrically charged. I could certainly feel it, as I had been feeling it for years. Up until then, I had no indication that she might be feeling it too.

At a certain moment, she leaned forward to put her glass back on the table. As she moved back toward me, it was too much for me to resist. My arm reached out to receive her as she came back, turning into my arms, and we kissed — a truly long, earth-moving kiss.

Her first words were, "Oh, honey. I'm so sorry. I can't believe I …My feelings for you …*How* could it happen?"

With that kiss, everything melted into one horrendous implosion. The dam was shattered, and eighteen years of pent-up passion poured out like water from a cracked glass jar. Too late — it couldn't be stopped, and what a relief for me. The words poured from me in a torrent. She was totally surprised and overwhelmed by the power of my words and her undeniable feelings for me. For the first time *ever*, I could finally say and express everything that had been bursting to be said. We spent the rest of the evening talking about what had just happened, how we were going to deal with it, and much kissing — *nothing more*. Anything more would just have to wait a year, since this revelation took place only a day before my leaving for home and a few days prior to my entering my first year at MIT. That, as you may well imagine, became perhaps the most difficult year of my life. MIT is not easy; classes go from nine to five every day and half days on Saturday for the first year. On registration day, assignments were included in the registration material — for assignments due on the first day of class. *Yikes!*

While Harvard students were sitting on the banks of the Charles River after perhaps a morning crib class, Tech men seem to be hard at work all day, every day, and long into the night.

"You can tell a Harvard man about a mile away because he looks, tsk, tsk, like he'd blow away, He always dresses in a pink chemise, he's got dimples on his rosy knees."

(Just kidding — that was just one of our beer drinking songs). Remember, Harvard's campus was only about a mile away from MIT. But I digress.

I pledged Sigma Chi fraternity and lived in the Sig house at 32 Beacon Street on the Back Bay Boston side of the Charles

River. I mention this in passing because my sophomore brothers were required to live in the house so they could be available to help freshmen with their difficult assignments. We had a curfew for freshmen in the house; otherwise they would study too late at night, trying to keep up with the homework. That extra attention and camaraderie helped get me through the first, very difficult year of nine-to-five classes five days a week and half days on Saturday Many freshmen, like me, had done well in high school without having to apply themselves; it came easily. But now things were entirely different and considerably more challenging. Add to that the fact that my mind was elsewhere. I managed to make it through that first of five years, had my preferred outdoor summer job doing construction work, and hitch-hiked back to Kansas City for my remaining vacation time.

As long as this unrequited love was on my part only, and I never spoke of it to anyone, I could deal with it. But once she and I both realized that she had the same feelings and we were so many miles apart, it was *excruciating* for the two of us. If it ever became known in our families, friendships and relationships would be blown apart—and she would, of course, be blamed. That was something I could not have tolerated because I knew that I was totally responsible. I had willed it. *I had made it happen.*

But the older woman is always held responsible. "She should never have *allowed* it to happen." "She knew better." "She should have seen it coming." "What was she thinking?" "That poor boy."

Right, ladies. But if you knew how happy she made "that poor boy" and how happy that poor boy made her feel, maybe you would consider giving it a try yourselves.

Step right up, ladies. Little do those critics understand the real power of love; it is not for everyone. When it happens, it is unstoppable, like a tidal wave that overtakes the mind as well as the body. I had never explored a female body—never felt a breast; a thigh; a beautiful, soft bottom; a smooth belly; a wet sex. And when I did, I was overcome. Yet it all came so naturally. I knew I had to go *there*, be *there*; and so I went *there*. Oh, how I went there. No experience just pure instinct, pure ecstasy. Strange as it may seem, the actual sex act was not the most important part of what was happening; it was being able to share the feeling — the *oneness*.

I believe that we only have one of these intense affairs possible within our minds and bodies. It is a piece of the soul that is available one time and is then gone — finished, *done*. Most people have never experienced it, though they may *think* they have. A classic FCA comment is, "I never thought it could be like this." Not that I wish it on anyone; it is difficult to deal with. It is all-consuming. Horrific crimes of passion are committed because of the intensity and hopelessness of some ultra-intense but impossible relationship.

There is a saying that I believe to be true: A major love affair is always followed by minor loves. It was certainly true in my case, as you will see. Is it being unfaithful to the true love? Not when the true love is an impossible love. Is it a desire to regain that wonderful feeling of excitement, even danger? Maybe to some extent that could play a role. Even when together with a minor love, the true love is always present — visually and even her perfume, her odor, her texture, and her taste. A true, impossible love, as opposed to just the first sexual experience, becomes a fantasy, always floating in the background.

It is never forgotten.

Of course, the impossibility of our situation was discussed at length. Marriage was not even considered. We realized that the age difference was not an insurmountable obstacle in itself. But we also realized that we could never live in the same city. We would not have been able to remain apart, avoid contact, and cover up the obvious feelings that radiated from our very demeanor. People can sense when love is in the air.

Women are quick to *get it* when one of their gang is in love. And eventually we would be found out. It was understood that I would finish my education and eventually find a partner somewhere in the future, somewhere in the world. But our feelings remained as strong as ever. We simply "banked the fire" as it were. We both knew this was for the best—the way it had to be—necessary for our situation, and it made life tenable.

Years later, my beautiful Brazilian wife, who knew my life's story in every detail, had the opportunity of meeting my first love, and the two spent some time together with her shortly before she passed away. They had no common language, but they had more than language in common. There was no jealousy—just a mutual understanding of loving as one.

Une Nouvelle Lune, 1980

Dis-moi Papa, ce truc-là.. non, *là, là-haut*.
On dirait une perle, un grelot, une gobille,
C'est rond, c'est joli, et ça luit… *Ah, je sais!*
C'est mon *bigarreau;* je l'ai perdu l'autre jour.

Le jour même où je faisais de grands sauts.
Tu sais comme je fais, de plus en plus haut.
Des fois je me donne le vertige, je le reconnais.

Mais chez nous c'est facile - on se sent si léger,

J'ai dit: "*regarde-moi*," mais tu étais occupé.
Tes yeux cherchaient l'espace, les étoiles, ou
qui sait.
Moi, je n'ai que cinq ans, mais je peux bien
imaginer
Un monde plein de gens, vivant sur ma bille
azurée.

Mais pourquoi as-tu choisi de l'appeler
Terre?
Puisqu'on voit bien que c'est suspendu dans
l'air.
Tandis que ma bille, que le soleil frôle au
loin,
Dans mon coeur sera pour nous, une
nouvelle lune.
Crois-tu qu'un jour, *oh! bien sûr!* pas demain,
Qu'il y aura des gens qui s'aiment, bien au
loin?
Eh bien soit! Les êtres que nous sommes…

Eh bien soit! Les êtres que nous sommes …

A New Moon

Tell me, Papa, that thing there—no *there, up high*.
It looks like a pearl, a bell clapper, a marble.
It's round, it's pretty and it shines. *Oh, I know!*
It's my *shooter*. I lost it the other day

The same day I was jumping so high.
You know how I do, higher and higher.
Sometimes I get dizzy,

I'll admit. But here it's easy we feel so light.

I called, "Watch me," but you were too busy.
Your eyes were searching space, whatever.

Me, I'm only five, but I can well imagine

A world full of people, living on a blue marble.

But why have you chosen to call it *Earth?*

When we can see it suspended in space.

While my marble that the sun caresses far
away,
In my heart will be for us, a new moon

Do you believe one day, *of course, not tomorrow*
There will be people who love, even out
there?
So be it! The beings, that we are …

Because *love* for us, is indispensable.

45

Chapter 8

My Fulbright Year

U pon graduation from MIT in 1956, with a Bachelor's Degree in Architecture, I was awarded a Fulbright grant for a year of study in Paris, France. "Study" meant carrying out a program that I had outlined in my Fulbright application, which was — travel to see architecture and, actively, to paint. As I explained in my application, I believe that an architect should be more than just an engineer — a builder of spaces within which human beings would function in various ways. But in addition, an architect should be well rounded in the plastic arts, painting, and other fine arts. Fine art drawing and painting had always been passions of mine, as was building huts, models, structures, and dwellings. So architecture seemed a likely combination of my various interests.

I had no idea how one should propose a program for a year abroad, in a way that would impress those whose job it would be to select recipients from the hundreds (thousands?) of applicants. I decided to be honest with myself (even though it might be looked at as a free vacation tour of Europe), to *not* promise an overambitious redesign of the world and so on, and to just take my chances. I felt that my references were as strong as I could hope for, as was my design portfolio. It is what it is, as they say.

The architecture department at MIT didn't rely solely on a permanent staff of professors and instructors but invited practicing architects to come to MIT as visiting lecturers for a school term or often a year or more. This gave students the opportunity to study under a wider variety of highly professional, experienced working architects from different parts of the United States and even foreign countries. I was fortunate to have profited from many of these professionals, such as Tobias Faber (professor and President of the Royal Danish Academy's School of Architecture) for one year. Toby had an ongoing practice in Copenhagen with his wife, Jytte, who was capable of holding down the fort in Copenhagen while Toby was away at MIT. Toby, in fact, became one of my professional references for the Fulbright Grant. Later, in my travels, I visited Toby and Jytte at their home in Copenhagen.

György Kepes, a Hungarian-born painter, photographer, and filmmaker who worked with the famous photographer Moholy-Nagy at the Bauhaus in Berlin and London and finally at the Chicago Institute of Design, believed, "Visual communication is universal and international; it knows no limits of tongue, vocabulary or grammar, and it can be perceived by the illiterate, as well as by the literate. The visual arts, as the optimum forms of the language of vision, are therefore an invaluable educational medium." He published a book, *Language of Vision* in 1944, which became, for many years, a college textbook. Other books authored by Kepes followed during his long career.

In 1947, he was invited to MIT to initiate a program in visual design — a division that later (ca 1968) became the Center for Advanced Visual Studies. When I first met him in 1952, I was impressed by his personality, his ideas, and his paintings. Besides my scheduled architectural and engineering courses, I found a couple of elective slots open, into which I could squeeze time to collaborate on projects with him. I remember well standing on a Boston street corner with my camera on a tripod snapping a single identical photo every hour on the hour over a twenty-four hour period for a project called, if my memory is correct, *The Image of the City*. As I look back at his and my paintings from the period, I can see his influence in my work from the fifties. Other than paintings I had on display in the Boston Young Painter's Gallery, Kepes became my principal painting critique. He too became one of my Fulbright Grant, professional references.

My application, combined with my professional and personal recommendations, a portfolio of architectural renderings and scale models, paintings, and sculpture went first to a professional committee of architects in New York for approval and then on to a government committee for approval and placement in my requested country — in this case, Paris, France.

What exactly is a Fulbright grant? Here is how *Wikipedia* describes it:

> "The Fulbright Program, including the Fulbright–Hays Program, is an American scholarship program of competitive, merit-based <u>grants</u> for <u>international educational exchange</u> for students, scholars, teachers, professionals, scientists and artists, founded by United States Senator J William Fulbright in 1946. On August 1, 1946, President Harry S. Truman signed the bill into law, and Congress created the Fulbright Program in what became the largest education exchange program in history.
>
> Under the Fulbright Program, competitively selected American citizens may become eligible for scholarships to study, conduct research, or exercise their talents abroad; and citizens of other countries may qualify to do the same in the United States of America. The program was established to increase mutual understanding between the people of the United States and other countries through the exchange of persons, knowledge, and skills. Candidates recommended for Fulbright grants have high academic achievement, a compelling project proposal and/or statement of

purpose, demonstrated leadership potential, and flexibility and adaptability to interact successfully with the host community abroad. It is one of the most prestigious scholarships in the world."

I was elated when I received notice that my application had been approved by the New York professional committee of architects and was on its way to Washington for approval and placement in a French Institution of higher learning. I felt that my professional and personal list of supporters deserved so much credit and personal thanks for vouching for my cause.

Of course, this all took time. I was in my fifth year (the Bachelor's Degree Architecture is a five-year program) when it was confirmed.

I had been awarded a Fulbright Grant for a one-year program in Paris, France.

Needless to say, I was ecstatic. All the extra work and the many nights I'd spent in the studio and the photo lab putting together a portfolio of work for my application had paid off. My dream had come true.

In September, I was to sail on the *Queen Mary* from New York to Cherbourg, France, and then on to Paris by boat train. *Wow!*

My parents drove me from Syracuse to New York City, along with several close friends to see me sail. My cabin mates were Garth and Bob, both Fulbright scholars and a padre whom I never did meet. The Atlantic crossing was rough—so rough, in fact, that the swimming pool was never filled and the dining tables had sideboards added to keep dishes from sliding off onto the floor. As the seas worsened, the tablecloths were wetted, and the tables and chairs were attached to the floor. Out of the six people at my table, I was finally the only one who never missed a meal. The others were fed apples and saltine crackers—the only food they could keep down.

The *Queen Mary*, with its three smokestacks, was like an old traditional English hotel—wood paneling everywhere.

Because of the rough seas, ropes were strung across large open areas for passengers to hold onto when attempting to cross and puddles of vomit could be found here and there, covered with sawdust until someone could clean them up. The crew recommended that passengers who suffered seasickness stay out on deck on the reclining deck chairs, where they could watch the horizon move up and down, rather than feeling that *they* were the ones who were moving up and down. It is very difficult to walk on a surface that is pitching and rolling, and one loses a visual horizon when inside. The inner ear loses control. But when it is very windy and the weather is chilly on deck, who wants to sit outside all bundled up in lap robes and blankets eating apples and saltine crackers? I personally have no problem with motion sickness, but I've heard from others that it is a most horrible feeling — the most debilitating, because there is no escape from the pitching and rolling until you reach port and terra firma, and even then you still stagger for a while.

The dance floor looked like a boxing ring, surrounded by taut ropes to keep the dancers from falling into the surrounding tables. The impression is that you are either ill or a bunch of drunks, laughing, staggering, and falling all over yourself and others.

On a cruise ship, it is said that the most entertainment always seems to be in the second and third class, so first class passengers go "slumming" for entertainment. We saw Liberace, his brother George (who was always with him), Noel Coward, and Kathryn Grayson regularly down in "steerage" with us in the evening. It was a memorable voyage — historic for me in many ways. It will certainly never be repeated.

Family and friends had come to see me off; it was very exciting, leaving one life behind and about to begin a whole new existence. I did not take this transformation lightly. On the first night out of New York, after lifeboat drill, we were all sitting at tables in the big activity room. It was crowded, but there was room at my table for two more people. In walked a cute Scottish mother with her nineteen-year-old daughter, on their way to Scotland for six months. I got up and offered them places at our table, which they accepted. My cabin mate chose the daughter, while I, of course, chose the mother. For the rest of the voyage, mother and I tried to find places to be alone (not easy, even on a ship as large as the *Queen Mary*). Mom was in an unhappy marriage; going back home to Scotland to think things over. Daughter was not happy about mother's high-seas affair, and to make matters worse, mother came to Paris *for a two-week stay*, which I did not need or encourage. It was her idea - her daughter was furious.

Paris — as far as I was concerned — was the heart of the world of painting, art, and fashion. But *politically* speaking, in 1956, France was fighting a colonial war in Algeria and was a key player in the Suez Crisis — *which meant gas rationing*. Was this going to hinder my program of European travel? My Volkswagen, ordered in New York, would be ready for pickup at the Wolfsburg factory within a couple of months. I was confident that it would all work out, as things always seemed to do. I assumed an attitude of, What? Me, worry?

The Fulbright grantees from the *Queen Mary* who landed in Cherbourg were directed to the boat train to Paris. Upon arrival in Paris, we were bused to the Cité Universitaire, a campus of country-sponsored student pavilions (dormitories) on the outskirts of Paris. It was all arranged by the Fulbright Commission for us to stay in the United States Pavilion for a week or so. There, we struck up friendships with fellow Fulbright scholars and even found partners to share living quarters, all while searching for permanent housing in Paris, preferably near the University of Paris, Sorbonne, area and learning to drink cheap wine. *We were students.* Our stipend was the equivalent of about $155 per month (in 1956, the official exchange rate was 350 French francs (FF) for 1 US dollar) and paid to us in French francs by the French government through the Fulbright Commission. We soon realized that it was doable, and it made us one with all the other students of the Left Bank, who came from all over the world, many from French colonies in West and North Africa. What a wonderful privilege we had been granted. We learned to be frugal, count our francs and centimes, buy one egg at a time, and do without heat or hot water. It's easy to see why I consider 1956/1957 to be a most important year of my life — a new country, new people, a new language, a new life.

Like a baby, it was a start from zero, though I had a lot of baggage in my back pocket, which would certainly come in handy. And I already knew how to walk.

Nevertheless, there were surprises. I remember well, one day I was walking the streets when I looked up and saw a large sign on a building that said "PCF, Parti Communiste Francais."*Whoa*, what's this?

Gee, maybe I should cross to the other side of the street just to be safe. As I later learned, PCF was just one of many political parties in France and quite legal. Actually, Paris was surrounded by what was known as the Red Belt of worker neighborhoods with low-cost housing (HLMs). It seems that a new political party springs up for every new dispute, schism, or political ideology. A week later, Garth and I decided to go see a political "protest" we'd heard about — something new to us. We took the Métro to the area where the protest was to take place. When we emerged from the Métro station, the streets seemed becalmed of physical movement, but we could hear distant commotion — yelling, the typical *pah paw, pah paw* horns of police cars. And as we wandered around, we noticed what appeared to be Red Cross emergency stations set up to treat the injured, complete with those military- type stretchers — just like in old wartime movies. There were some cobblestones (pavés) and mini barricades strewn around indicating that a battle of some sort had occurred right there where we were standing, which created a feeling of apprehension in me. Throughout

French history, the classic cobblestone was the projectile of choice. Streets were paved with them, so they were always plentiful. They were laid in a characteristic pattern without mortar or grout—just tapped into a base of sand. Once you dig out the first stone, then the rest come easily; just pick up and heave. Cobblestones have pretty much disappeared from city streets now. The cast-iron grates around tree bases were readily available for making barricades to block the streets.

Suddenly from a side street, a gang of protesters, maybe two hundred strong, came running around the corner toward us making a lot of noise, in French of course, followed by police in helmets, shields, and whaling sticks. *Uh-oh*. What to do? Fight or flight? A quick decision was needed. *Holy crap*, it took but a second for us to go from "innocent bystanders" to "fleeing protesters." If we ran, we became one of them. But if we just stood there, we were stupid and sure to get a bloodied head and a night *en tôle* (detained) And for what cause? We didn't even know what the protest was about—*duh!* Luckily, we managed to escape into another *bouche* de Métro and made our way to safety. We did learn something though. Political demonstrations and protests are *not* spectator sports. There are no "innocent bystanders." If you are there, you are a participant and subject to getting hurt.

On November 23, I was driven home from a French class in a chauffeur- driven car by the wife of the Bolivian ambassador to France (he would eventually become the short-term president of Bolivia). I had met Rosa Elena days before in the class, and we had become friends—often having coffee at the Alliance Française. They were moving to a new apartment on Ave. President Wilson, and I was invited to several receptions at their residence. On November 22, we had another reception for Senator Fulbright and his wife. It seemed champagne was flowing from all sides.

I received a telegram from Wolfsburg that my car was ready. I was expected in Wolfsburg by 11:00 am on November

24 — night train to Braunschweig, taxi to Wolfsburg, and I arrived fifteen minutes early. Such efficiency; no clumsy bureaucracy here! Rapid paperwork, insurance paid, title in hand, a photo of my powder blue VW at the end of the assembly line. And I was off to Paris.

Now, back to my program — travel to see architecture and, actively, to paint. Fulbright recipients were expected to notify the commission about travel plans outside of our respective countries — not as a means of control but simply so they had an idea of our whereabouts.

Having met so many students in such a short time, I found it easy to find others eager to share expenses for travel around Europe by car. I had three circuits in mind — (1) Iberia (Spain and Portugal); (2) Europe (including Yugoslavia, Greece over to Istanbul, and Turkey); and (3) Scandinavia (Denmark, Norway, Finland, and Sweden). I had determined that gas rationing should not be a problem outside of France, as long as I applied for ration tickets when and where necessary. Within France, I was allowed thirty liters (about eight US gallons) per month, since my car had the German Z tourist license plate. Somehow I managed to get an extra ninety liters in ration tickets at the prefecture for my first trip — easily enough to get us to the Spanish border. That, plus exchanging currency (both official and unofficial rates) made travel in those days even more exciting, if somewhat more dangerous. There was always an unofficial (black market) rate to be found somewhere — when you are shopping for fifty-cent hotel rooms, eating pâté, fruit, and wine by the side of the road, in parks, or on beaches, and drinking the cheapest table wine available (which, in fact, you observe the townspeople buying for everyday consumption). When in Rome.

For my first of three big trips, we had placed an ad at the American Express in Paris and found two English students wanting a ride as far as Madrid and perhaps on to Lisbon. In those days, American Express was the home away from home for American students, hitchhikers and backpackers who had no fixed addresses. It was the equivalent of the French *Poste Restante*. Letters, boxes, and the like could be sent to them in major cities, for eventual pickup by the student, or messages could simply be posted on bulletin boards, to be seen by all travelers. Word always managed to get around. "Hey, I saw your name on the notice board in Athens. Did you get the message?"

On December 21, we left for Spain, making Bordeaux the first night. We found a hotel, worked out a price, continued driving around looking for something cheaper, and decided the first hotel was the best deal. But then we couldn't find that same hotel again. Oh well….

On to Biarritz first thing in the morning. It was a beautiful coastal town, and we had breakfast there, then into Spain, to San Sebastian, where we tried to change francs for pesetas. We found that we could do better in France, so we drove *back* twelve miles to the border, left the car, and walked across the border into France. After buying pesetas, we walked back across into Spain and my car. (Sounds dumb I know, but a penny saved really was a penny earned to us.)

Similar scenarios trying to save money occurred many times during our travels; we can laugh about them today.

We drove to Deva along the coast and then on to Bilbao, which was not very interesting. But we bought bread, olives, and tomatoes and ate by the side of the road. Continuing on toward Burgos, we passed through beautiful mountains and high vertical cliffs and photographed two charming villages nestled between mountains. Donkey carts seemed to be the major means of transportation. Burgos was one of my target places to visit because of its important *high* Gothic cathedral, Our Lady of Burgos, started in 1221 and completed in 1567. Due to the over four-century history of construction, including a two-century hiatus, it stands today as a comprehensive example of the evolution of Gothic style. While we were exploring the cathedral, the choir was practicing. Choral singing echoing through a Gothic cathedral will always send shivers through me. I wanted to linger longer. The cathedral became a UNESCO World Heritage Site in 1984.

Rather than arrive in Madrid late in the day, we decided to spend the night in Aranda de Duero, a small town north of Madrid—a decision that provided unexpected but most interesting results. We found the hotel Ibarra to our liking and budget, checked in, and did what all Spaniards do in the evening; we walked around town. The townspeople do it because their evening meal is taken late, and they stay outside while waiting for their houses to cool down from the high daily temperatures.

A gentleman approached us, and we talked to him for a while. Seems he was a dentist, and he asked us to meet him at a specific café at 7:30; he would bring some young townspeople people who spoke some English. This we did, and an interesting evening commenced. They were interested in life in America, what we studied, how we lived, and so on. Of course, they all dreamed of visiting the United States. Coffee and Spanish cognac flowed (beer at seven cents a glass, Cognac at six cents a glass). Then they took us to a local town dance, where more curious young people swarmed around us. We were the town attraction that night, but it was clear that Aranda de Duero was not a hot tourist attraction by any means. What a wonderful night; I still have a clay ashtray from the hotel in my collection.

At 9:30 the next morning, we were on our way to Madrid, arriving about noon. We found a cheap hotel and walked the streets, appalled at the number of beggars—women with babies and small children; it was pitiful. We did the sights, including the Cité Universitaire of Madrid; ate dinner at 11:00pm; and went to bed. The next evening, we went to a popular Flamenco theater, which began at 11:00, and the show finished at 2:00am Seems a crazy way to live.

On December 27, we left Madrid for Lisbon by way of Toledo. Toledo is known as the Imperial City (because it was the seat of Charles V, the Holy Roman Emperor) and the City of Three Cultures because of the historical coexistence of Christians, Jews, and Muslims. A small town marked by the palace/fortress of the Alcázar on one hilltop and the Gothic cathedral on another, Toledo, on the whole, was a feast for the eyes.

The cathedral alone is worth a long visit because of the paintings by Goya, Titian, Bellini, Van Dyck, Raphael and Zubarán, and Rubens, plus eighteen El Greco paintings — an incredible treasure. El Greco's masterpiece, *The Burial of the Count of Orgaz*, hangs in an annex of the church of Santo Tomé. It pained me to see tourists wasting time on frivolous souvenir shopping in Toledo when so many incredible art treasures are available for the public to see and appreciate.

We made Lisbon in one long day from Toledo, arriving late evening. Tired as we were, we ended up in a *fado* club, which was most interesting, being that the music form was unknown to us. Fado is a very melancholic music. Songs can be about almost any subject (broken hearts, loneliness, death), and the music itself is sad and mournful. The Portuguese, being men of the sea, love songs about sea farers years away from home or often never returning from long voyages. Phrasing by fado singers is unusual — unique to the genre but really quite beautiful.

We toured Lisbon, did Sintra for dinner, headed south to the Algarve, crossed back into Spain, and headed on toward Sevilla and Algeciras, one of the largest ports in Europe, from which we were taking a ship to Tangiers, Morocco.

We arrived late afternoon of December 30 and found another cheap hotel (Hotel Fuentes) in the old city by the port. It was rather gruesome but exotic in a picturesque sort of way, much like the films from the 1940s set in the Kasbah of Tangiers. Sidney Greenstreet, where are you? This was a time warp — veiled women and men in wrinkled white linen suits. We discovered that we got an electric shock if we touched the running water in our room.

We walked and shopped, got caught in a torrential rainstorm, packed, and paid our hotel bill. It came to 130 pesetas each (about $2.65) for two nights and three meals — which justified my "gruesomely exotic but picturesque" choice.

We took a ship to Gibraltar and then a ferry to Algeciras, picked up the car, and headed for Granada to visit the Alhambra, a Moorish palace, and then on to Malaga. We bought ham, bread, tomatoes, and fruit juice and ate in the car. We found a reasonable hotel in Malaga but no hot water until 10:00am, so we slept in, waiting for hot water and some much-needed baths. Then we headed on to Almeria, where we found rooms for fifty cents a night, ate dinner, walked around town, and crashed, knowing we had about a 480-kilometer drive to Valencia the next day.

During the next day's drive, we passed the highest point in Spain — a mountain in the Sierra Nevada, which was snow covered, as were other peaks in the region. The coast of Spain is very beautiful but spotted with very poor villages along the way. The country is rocky, with agricultural plots scratched out of the poor soil in unlikely locations on hillsides but always near the ubiquitous cave dwellings that pockmarked the cliffs. The next night, we found a decent hotel in Valencia for thirty-one pesetas — a bit over our usual cheap room rate, but it was located right on the town square and offered hot water, and those qualities bring a higher premium every time, of course.

On January 3, we arrived in Barcelona after having seen a major highway accident — a donkey cart tipped over into the ditch. Something we had not fully realized is that, when a donkey cart tips over into a ditch, the donkey *also* tips over into the ditch. An upside down donkey cart is one thing, but an upside down donkey is quite another; and besides, the donkey was *not* happy. Upside down donkeys are quite likely to kick the snot out of anyone who approaches. The problem was finally resolved. The donkey survived, as did the cart, and we continued on our way to Barcelona, eating apples, tangerines, and bananas along the way. I was excited to be approaching Barcelona — the mother lode of architectural interest for me. We found a cheap hotel for thirty pesetas each and had a good dinner for eighteen and half pesetas — right on budget.

Now for a wonderful day with Antoni Gaudi (1852–1926), the architect responsible for some of the most unusual architectural expressions of modern times. Gaudi's work, based on organic forms and often embellished with broken pieces of ceramic pottery, uses an unusual approach to structure, employing *catenary* curves structurally, eliminating the need for buttresses, as had been necessary in the neo-Gothic style. This creates an entirely unexpected original look to the spires and structure of the Church of the Sacred Family or Sagrada Familia, eliciting such comments as, "What holds it up?" On the other hand, it makes life difficult for follow-up architects and builders responsible for interpreting what Gaudi intended after his death. Construction of the church was begun in 1882, but when Gaudi died in 1926, the church was said to be less than a quarter complete. There were no drawn plans, working drawings, or engineering drawings for the builders to follow. Gaudi worked with models and sketches and detailed hand-drawn perspectives. There were few straight lines in his concept; everything followed natural forms, like trees and branches — a difficult task for those responsible for realizing Gaudi's dreams.

The building program has always depended entirely on donations. After Gaudi's death, his work and reputation suffered considerable neglect. Along came the Spanish Civil War from 1936 to 1939, which didn't help. And of course, there were always detractors of Gaudi's work. It was during the 1950's that Gaudi's reputation was on the rise, and it has continued to increase almost to a saintly status ever since.

The projected date for completion is 2026, but I have my doubts. In 2010, Pope Benedict XVI consecrated it a *"minor basilica."* It deserved more than that.

It was time for me to study this man and his creations in more detail. We visited his wonderful park and all of his playful apartment facades.

We headed for the border at Millau, where we once again applied for gas rationing tickets at the prefecture. They gave us 120liters (31 gallons), which would get us to Paris easily by January 5, 1957. Our total mileage for the trip was well over 4,000miles.My out-of-pocket for the entire trip was under $100 for *everything*, including some gift shopping.

We planned our next trip of the trilogy for some time in April. In the meantime, I was painting, gallery hopping, and attending any painting exhibition and vernissages (show openings) open to the public (and some which were not); and in Paris, there are many.

I require stimulation, both visual and intellectual, if I am to be creative. The idea of being on a desert island with a canvas and some paint, thinking that great works will be forthcoming is utter nonsense. Nothing would be produced. Why bother? I need activity, people, visual stimulation, music, art, conversation. Every afternoon I spent on the rue de Beaune or the rue des Beaux Arts, the rue de Seine or the rue Bonaparte, hopping from one gallery to the next. I was overwhelmed by the amount of art and how it made me want to rush home and create — often all night long. Did I think it as all *great* art? Time will probably determine that. What was important was that someone created it; it was real, as it stood there to be seen. Who is to decide if it is *great* art at the time it is created? Even the painter doesn't know or care if what he has painted is *good*. It takes time to ripen, to mature. I know because I paint. Time will tell — *maybe*.

I was using a unique medium at that time — a medium that I and a Japanese painter had developed while at MIT.

We found that a DuPont product called Hypalon was soluble in turpentine. We could make it to a desired consistency, combine it with oil paints and even metallic powders, and achieve interesting results.

I had taken enough to Paris to last several years by having a quantity dissolving at any given time; it was a slow, tedious process. Years later, I discovered acrylics in the United States and found the results to be very similar.

While gallery-hopping one day, I dropped into Raymond Duncan's workshop. Raymond was the brother of Isadora Duncan, the famous modern dancer who died when a long scarf wrapped itself around the axle of a speeding open car and strangled her to death. I walked past his gallery/workshop on the rue de Seine almost daily. The door was always open, and I would see him dressed in his usual Greek togas, always diligently working over something (though I never knew *what* exactly). He was a most interesting personage. He was usually there, so one day I entered, introduced myself and we chatted for a while. He always had time to chat.

In Paris, there is stimulation at every turn and in every doorway, both visually and intellectually.

Marcel Brion (a French essayist, historian, art and literary critic, and my Fulbright advisor) had been following my work. He said of my paintings, "They should be seen." He felt that I should try to have a show and recommended that I contact the Gallery de Beaune, which I did. Madame Suzanne de Coninck, who owned the gallery, kept one of my paintings and immediately put it in the gallery window. By that time, I was painting in a large studio under the eaves at the American Club, Blvd. Raspail in Montparnasse.

This was a large old house in a park-like setting, surrounded by walls — what the French would call a *propriété*. Cultural events, lectures, performances, and tea dances plus a wonderful, inexpensive restaurant made this a popular hangout for foreign students. I could paint in the large open studio any time of the day or evening along with other artists. I was still experimenting with Hypalon, doing nonobjective paintings.

One of the other painters, Peter Saul, a young American painter, eventually made it big in the art world and is now considered one of the fathers of the pop art movement. Back then, he was very quiet, keeping pretty much to himself in a corner of the studio, slathering great gobs of paint on his colorful canvasses depicting such things as jukeboxes, automobiles, and other familiar objects. We heard that he was supported by a sponsor. There was no doubt in our minds that this guy was different. But isn't that what art is about anyway?

Painting, buying canvasses and painting supplies, and applying for gas tickets almost caused me forget that, for our next trip, we would need visas for crossing Yugoslavia. We made the applications, and the visas were ready for pickup on April 11.

For this trip, we had found two girls willing to cram into my powder blue VW with minimum baggage each and head south—no romantic interests at all, just friends sharing expenses. Three of us were Fulbright scholars, plus Yolanda, a sweet young girl who wanted to see the world. So why not with us?

Of course that didn't last long. Love had to enter into the mix to complicate our lives (but it did eventually lead to a marriage, though not between Yolanda, or Yoyo, and me; as you know by now if you've been paying attention, she was much too young for my taste). But we did stick to our original plan—the two guys in one room, the two gals in another, for the entire trip, in spite of the romance brewing in our midst. Most people could foresee problems with this setup immediately. In fact, the second female soon became known as *Her Highness*, spoiled like you wouldn't believe.

On Saturday, April 13, we picked up Yoyo, the group had breakfast together, and we got under way by 8:00am We headed toward the Côte d'Azur but had an important side trip to make over near the Swiss border at Ronchamp, to visit Le Corbusier's Chapelle Notre-Dame du Haut—often cited as one of the century's most important buildings. It was completed in 1954, about three years before our visit, so the paint would hardly be dry. On first sight from a distance, it appeared to be a chapel of moderate size. But as we got closer, it grew visually to become a very large, quite striking shape, resembling a ship plowing the ocean. The soaring roof, curved walls, and unusual spaces they created were unexpected for modernist Le Corbusier. I found it to be somewhat whimsical. However, I did not care for the bright red painted walls in one chapel or the violet wall in the sacristy. My instinct as an architect was in conflict with the painter in me.

We made it to Avignon, filled the tank using only one ration ticket, found the necessary two rooms ($2.20 each), and had dinner ($.85 each, wine included). The next day, we visited the Notre-Dame cathedral and the papal palace. And we danced on the famous Pont d'Avignon ruins jutting half way across the Rhône River, singing, *"Sur le pont d'Avignon l'on y danse, l'on y danse"* and taking silly photos. Between 1309 and 1377 seven successive popes occupied the papal palace, which is why that period is known as the Avignon Papacy. The popes held control until 1791, when, during the French Revolution, Avignon again became part of France. The original Roman city has preserved its medieval ramparts.

From Avignon, we headed for Marseilles—not that I was interested in the city itself. But another building on my list of "things not to miss" was another of Le Corbusier's renowned works, *Cité Radieuse*—an enormously heavy-looking concrete building; more like a massive sculpture than a building to be lived in by humans.

Le Corbusier's famous axiom, "A house is a machine to live in," can certainly be applied here, if we consider this building to be a "machine," ignoring *my* personal philosophy that a living space must respect the human scale, which this building does not. I understand that it was considered an experiment at the time — to include shopping streets on every third floor, a hotel, and a gymnasium. It would be a self-contained vertical city of 337 modular apartments. What shocked me *inside*, was the uncomfortable volumes, spaces, and rooms, probably dictated by the constraints of the modular system employed. Apartments had rooms that were strange in their proportions — ceilings too high for the width or length of a room. When sitting on the balcony (every unit had one), a large, heavy horizontal concrete beam crossed directly at eye level of someone sitting down, thus blocking the view. The building sat on enormous, oversized pylons big enough to support Atlas himself *and* his world. I have read that the excuse for the enormous pylons was that, because of a shortage of reinforcing steel, they had to be more massive — in other words, more concrete. *Really?*

Certainly, it was a critical disappointment for me. But who was I to judge? I had seen many photos of it without realizing how disappointed I would eventually be. I'm glad I went out of my way to see it.

Finally, we had reached the Côte d'Azur and Nice, where we found a hotel with a small kitchen in one of our rooms. The girls got the room with the kitchen so we could prepare our meals during our stay in Nice. We prepared our lunches in the room but ate on the beach. We stacked the dishes in the bidet; made a small sign, "Another Fulbright First," and took pictures of the setup.

We scrounged more gas ration tickets by saying we needed them to get to Paris. But of course we intended to continue along the French Riviera to Cannes, Monaco and into Italy. We continued along the Italian Riviera to Finale Ligure and on to Genoa, Santa Margherita and Portofino - all gorgeous Mediterranean towns that beckon one to stay a while, relax, and just take it easy. (Years later, I returned to Finale Ligure several times while on vacation in the South of France.)

We stayed at the Pensione Appiani in Santa Margherita for $1.10 each. Then I began my "spaghetti Bolognese" *cure.* I love that stuff. Though pasta is usually only one course of a multicourse Italian meal, I would often simply order two plates of pasta, not only because it would usually be the cheapest dish (remember our budget), but also because I can never get enough. Finale Ligure also rests in my memory as the place where I ate the very best lasagna ever, though that was many years later.

Now to Pisa, where of course we climbed the leaning tower well before the Italians began to worry that it was about to tumble over. It was closed to climbers for many years while they fretted over how to save it from falling. Anyway, I returned years later and by golly, it is still standing.

Then came Florence — *the magnificent city* (my words). Florence, OMG treasures everywhere; they're all around, just stroll with open eyes (and a good guidebook so you don't overlook anything). I was always impressed by the simple urinals set into the walls of buildings for the convenience of men. How thoughtful and practical those Italians.

The Italians say you are either a Roman or a Florentine — an easy choice for me. I'm a Florentine all the way. After all, this was where the Renaissance began, where Michelangelo sculpted, where Brunelleschi designed the dome. It's the home of Giotto's bell tower, Ghiberti's *Gates of Paradise,* the Florence Baptistery, Cathedral Santa Maria del Fiore, and Vasari's *Last Supper.* The wondrous treasures never seemed to end — yet they almost did.

Fast-forward to November 1966 — the year the Arno overflowed during the worst flood Florence had ever experienced.

After several days of torrential rain, the Arno River could not handle the rush of water from the mountains, and it overflowed its banks. Millions of rare books, manuscripts, paintings, fine art, and frescoes were destroyed or damaged. Thousands of families were left homeless. Thousands of businesses were forced to close. Tons of mud, heating oil, sewage, and detritus destroyed building interiors, as well as their priceless content. Try to imagine the Last Supper painting *under water for twelve hours.*

When I read about it in Paris, I was heartsick. I visited Florence a couple of years after the catastrophe and could clearly see the high-water marks on buildings several feet above my head. Restoration is still ongoing, and will be for years. I was told an anecdote by a Florentine, which I can believe is true and is common knowledge anyway. The famous Ponte Vecchio (shopping bridge over the Arno River) was the only bridge in Florence not destroyed by the Germans in World War II. People rushed to see if the Ponte Vecchio was still standing, feeling that "if that bridge withstood the war, it could withstand the flood" — and it did.

With the combined effort of Italian and foreign volunteers alike, called *angeli del fango* ("mud angels"), many of these fine works have been and are still being restored. But decades later, much work remains to be done.

When Florence commemorated the fiftieth anniversary of the flood in 2016, it unveiled the reinstallation of possibly the most famous work to have been severely damaged and saved — Vasari's five-panel painting of the Last Supper. Other masterpieces that were damaged included Cimabue's great Crucifix at Santa Croce, and Donatello's *Penitent Magdalene.*

The Florence flood of 1966 can never be forgotten. We should all shed a tear in silence.

After searching around Florence, we came up with a three-room apartment on the top floor of a hotel. With two bedrooms (four beds), a sitting room, and a bathroom with a shower for 100 lire (about $1.60) per night, per person and located near the *Duomo*, (Cathedral Santa Maria del Fiore). It was wonderful.

We planned on driving to Rome on April 19, realizing how difficult it would be to find lodging due to Easter. We stopped by the American Academy, but there was no space available. However, the secretary arranged for us to stay where she herself stayed — again for 100 lire apiece. We saw the illuminated sites by night, pretty much following the guidebook. I must say, Rome was somewhat of a disappointment — too big, too dirty, and too much crazy traffic. Each point of interest floated loose in a sea of "city," totally isolated one from the other — a lack of continuity. Florence, on the other hand, is an integrated fine arts history book into which one sinks as in a warm, unctuous bath of pure artistic sensuality. Going directly from Florence to Rome is probably not the right way to do it. The reverse order makes more sense to me.

We did St. Peter's on Easter Sunday of course and saw the Pope come out on his balcony. He seemed to be looking directly at me when he waved. (Do you suppose he recognizes a sinner when he sees one? Or a saint? Probably not.) After that experience, I was ready for my two plates of spaghetti for lunch. It really freaks out the waiters when I repeat one after the other that way.

Then we did the Appian Way, the Catacombs of San Sebastiano, the Church of Quo Vadis, the graves of Keats and Shelley in the protestant cemetery, the Pyramid Cestius, the Basilica of Santa Maria Maggiore, and the Basilica of Santa Maria del Popolo. We finished the day by returning to St. Peters to see the Vatican by night.

I was still chasing down leads to a possible architectural job in Rome. I had several names of recommended architects and professors, but around Easter, they seemed to be unavailable.

After a couple of days in Rome, my opinion hadn't changed — wonderful things to see but lacking a coherent atmosphere such as I find in Paris. Paris is Paris everywhere; Rome is historic site to historic site. Florence is a gem.

On our way out of Rome, we visited EUR (Esposizione Universale Roma), the site of Mussolini's 1942 world's fair, which never took place due to World War II. I was interested in Italy's neoclassic Fascist architecture, which I knew was featured in several films by Fellini and even a 1999 adaptation of Shakespeare's *Titus Andronicus*.

It's a hodgepodge of austere buildings along axially laid out streets. The Palazzo de la Civiltà Italiana (Colesseo Quadrato), with its facades of deep- cut, arched niche windows designed to each eventually house a piece of sculpture, is the most widely known example of Fascist architecture in Italy. To me, it has become a caricature of the Fascist style.

We continued on south to Naples and decided to drive to the top of Vesuvius before searching for a hotel. The drive up the mountain took us through areas of terrible poverty. Hordes of people were streaming down the mountain on foot, coming from a huge fiesta picnic at the top. Adorable but dirty children sang and danced along the way, begging for coins and cigarettes.

We found lodging in Vico Equense (Pensione Aequa), a part of Naples near Pompeii, for 600 lire each. The outdoor patio overlooked orange groves, the Bay of Naples, Vesuvius, and the blue Mediterranean. On Tuesday, April 23, we toured the ruins of Pompeii. Imagining what horrors took place the day Pompeii literally disappeared under tons of ash and cinders, reminds one that it can erupt again at any time. When we arrived at the famous Pompeii brothel with the "advertising" wall paintings, the caretakers would not allow Yoyo or Her Highness to enter.

After lunch on the patio of our pension, we headed south for one of the most beautiful coastal drives in the world — the Amalfi Coast, a fifty- kilometer drive that includes Sorrento, Positano, Amalfi, and on to Salerno. The drive is indescribable but slow moving due to the curves and dangerous cliffs above the sea and the snail's pace of rubbernecking tourists. But with so much beautiful scenery to see, we simply rubbernecked with the best of them.

Each time I look at a place like Amalfi, I think it is the most beautiful view in the world. Then I look at Positano, and I think the same thing again. Then I look at …and I think the same thing again. Every person on this planet should have the opportunities I have had, and am continuing to have, to witness such incredible beauty — where man has worked with nature, resulting in these breathtaking results.

From Salerno, we crossed Italy to Foggia. We had a crazy Russian hotel in Foggia — four beds in one room, with a chamber pot under each bed but… cheap! Lots of laughs that night.

We made Venice the next day, arriving after dark. The Adriatic coastal drive is not very difficult or scenic, so we made good time to Venice. We parked the car in the parking garage (can't drive in Venice because the streets are flooded) and boarded a waterbus to the Piazza San Marco, got off the boat, and just stood in *awe*. The piazza was beautifully illuminated — café's bustling, orchestras playing, people strolling. It couldn't be real; it was pure theater — *a dream sequence.*

At that moment, Yo and I both had the same thought. *I shouldn't be here; this is not right for this moment. I should turn around, leave Venice, and only return at some later day with the love of my life.*

Yo and I spent time walking and talking about life in general, our other relationships, her French boyfriend, and this rather unique travel arrangement, while the lovebirds wandered off by themselves.

(I lost track of Yolanda upon our return to Paris, but I was able to return to Venice for the second time as I had hoped to, forty-nine years later in 2006 with my beautiful Brazilian wife, after thirty-one years of marriage by that time. And lo and behold, the Piazza was again beautifully illuminated and orchestras were playing. Let me imagine that it was all staged just for our belated honeymoon. One big difference though — in 2006, we stayed at the five-star Hotel Danieli. I certainly hope that Yolanda was able to realize a similar dream.)

We stayed at the Albergo Stella d'Oro e Bella Vista for 900lire per person for our usual two rooms, and it featured "running water, central heating, great family cuisine, and low prices." How could we go wrong? Plus, it was only a block off the Piazza San Marco. We did the sites for a couple of days — in other words, fed the pigeons, listened to the orchestras in the evening, climbed the Campanile, visited the basilicas, art galleries, and art exhibitions and got lost many times wandering around while crossing most of the four hundred bridges of Venice — like the average tourists we were happy to become.

On April 26, we got up early, bought sandwiches for the trip, picked up the car, and headed for Trieste. I hated to leave Venice, away from automobile traffic, a whole other world. But we had other worlds to conquer. Considering the world political situation at that time, we decided to drive across Yugoslavia as the best way to get to Greece and Turkey by car, instead of putting the car on a ship.

Entering Yugoslavia, we were limited as to currency we were allowed to bring in. We hid money in a thermos bottle. We crossed the border of Yugoslavia about dark and drove to Zagreb. We passed through a mountainous area and noticed a very bright comet with what appeared to be two tails, just hanging in the sky in front of the car. We, of course, had no way of verifying what we were seeing, but all four of us saw it quite clearly. We were traveling southward and saw the comet for several nights — almost all the way to Athens, Greece.

We found a hotel in Zagreb and took two rooms as was our habit, for about $1.50 per person. The city was very quiet. With no traffic, it seemed ghostlike.

I made a point of writing down the date and our location in my diary to pinpoint the comet, thinking that someday I could research and identify it specifically.

Many years later, I researched comets and found exactly what I was looking for. That well-documented but very new comet carries the name Arend–Roland, "discovered on November 8, 1956 by S. Arend and G. Roland of Belgium. In April 1957, near the perihelion, it attained the brightness of a star of the first stellar magnitude." To us it was very bright and prominent in the sky for several days. The comet could be observed by telescope until April 1958. Another article said it would not return for several million years. We decided we couldn't wait.

The countryside was flat as far as Belgrade, and the roads were good. We found another hotel with a great dinner included for 400 dinars per person. The meal consisted of grilled pork chops with mashed potatoes, gravy, salad, brown bread, and beer.

We entered Yugoslavia with 15,500 dinars (about $25) purchased in Trieste. We figured that should be enough to get us into Greece without changing more money, remembering that any dinars we had left over would be worthless outside of Yugoslavia.

There were posters of Maréchal Tito everywhere, the hammer and sickle on every wall and soldiers stationed throughout the towns and cities to remind us that we were in a Communist, possibly non-friendly country. Any kind of control could divulge our having crossed into Yugoslavia with too many illegal dinars, since we did not change any money *after* crossing the border as required by law. And 15,500 dinars was an enormous stack of paper money, some of which we hid in a thermos bottle between the glass insert and the outer shell. We were lucky; nothing transpired.

South of Belgrade the roads deteriorated seriously, and we assumed they would get worse into Greece. Now we were driving on dirt roads, but the scenery was spectacular.

By night the comet was still leading us on, hanging in the sky like a painting on a wall. Traveling four in a small car, deep in a not-so-friendly foreign country, and far from civilization and electricity, it seemed as if we were huddled in a kind of powder blue space capsule, hurtling through darkest space, and being drawn toward a rendezvous with a comet? Yes, it was eerie and somewhat scary. We were not looking to make headlines.

The next day, April 28, we had lunch in a small roadside restaurant. People were poor but extremely friendly. The typical cuisine had a decidedly German influence. The owner took us into the kitchen so we could point to whatever food appealed to each of us for lunch, as we had no common language. It was a delightful experience, and the food was excellent. The people were very peasant-like and obviously people of the land. The women looked to be hard-working and strong. The oxcart seemed to be the principal work vehicle, hauling building material, dirt from a river bottom, and everything having to do with farming. Everyone was curious and extremely friendly, especially the children. There was obviously no tourism whatsoever; few automobiles were on the roads or in the cities. The Dalmatian coast had yet to be discovered by Europeans as a very inexpensive but very beautiful vacation destination. I wish we had known more about its potential at the time. We might have tried a coastal route instead of cutting right down through the center of the country. But that would have meant a slow, underdeveloped, difficult route well off the beaten path, and Greece was calling to us. We simply chose to use Yugoslavia as a way of getting to Greece and Turkey by car.

So, we left dinars behind and adopted drachmas as our new currency when we crossed into Greece at about 5:00 pm, continuing on to Kozani for the night and our first Greek food. Again, we went into the kitchen and pointed (this round was not so good — too much strong mutton for my taste) and shared another single room with four beds. You can't win them all, I guess; but on our travel budget, you accepted becoming one big happy family.

From the border to Kozani, we climbed a very high mountain pass, which we assumed was beautiful. We couldn't see in the dark. However we knew it was dangerous, that there were no guardrails, and that Greeks were atrocious drivers. Approaching oncoming cars, we found the drivers would blink their headlights several times and then *turn their lights off entirely* at the very moment of passing. Try *that* on a winding mountain road sometime.

Here again, everyone took to the streets after dinner, plus the wagons, bicycles, scooters, and carts — all with no lights or reflectors of any kind. We could still see our comet, though it wasn't as bright. We intended to drive to Athens the following day (April 29) so that would probably be the end of our comet because of the expected bright city lights.

We did make Athens before dark, having crossed four or five mountain chains on the way. It was very beautiful scenery with many charming villages. We stopped in one to watch a traveling circus with two bears, a monkey and musicians playing. I identified them as gypsies due to their dress, but my goodness, were they ever filthy dirty.

We approached Athens, almost at sundown. We could see the Acropolis far away on its hilltop, illuminated by the setting sun. What a perfect introduction to the history we were about to become immersed in.

Athens was as I expected — hot, dirty, dusty, and noisy. The smell of food emanated from every doorway and window. Athens seemed overactive — until siesta time when pretty much everything stopped. We settled for the Hotel Estia Emboron, not only with a view of the Acropolis (easy to say because the Acropolis could be seen from just about anywhere since it sat on one of Athens seven hills) but also within walking distance. We had a fine dinner in the hotel. I was in heaven because my spaghetti was only $.50 a plate. So of course I had two — one as my appetizer and the second as my main dish, not an easy thing to explain to a Greek-only-speaking waiter. The hotel was the most expensive of our trip so far, at almost $5 per person, breakfast included. You only live once.

Athens demanded intensive sightseeing and should be done on foot. How else could you explore the Plaka with its taverns and restaurants? Or you could find a good bus tour with all the little old Midwestern ladies in tennybumpers, being dragged along by their oversized shoulder bags.

"C'mon, Mabel, stop looking at those pornographic ashtrays; we'll be late for lunch."

We left Athens at about 9:30am, early (for us), with the intention of making Thessaloniki (Greece's second largest city, 570kilometers away, by evening — which we did. We took in more beautiful scenery populated by goats, sheep, donkey carts, farmers, children, and the like. We found another very reasonable hotel ($3 apiece) and excellent food for less than a dollar in a restaurant across the street from the hotel.

We hoped to make Istanbul the next day, May 3 (a journey of about 796kilometers) if all went well. After lunch in a small café in Alexandroupoli, we changed $20 each to Turkish lire at 9 lire for $1(though the official rate was 5.25lire for $1) for incidentals and eventual gift shopping. We stopped in a small Greek fishing village, the last Greek town just before crossing into Turkey. The fishermen and townspeople gathered around, wanting their pictures taken with us. It was a wonderful, friendly sendoff from Greece.

It was now late in the day. We had just crossed the border to Edirne, situated 7 kilometers from the Greek and 20 kilometers from the Bulgarian border.

Edirne is famed for its many mosques, domes, and minarets. It served as the third capital of the Ottoman Empire before Constantinople (Istanbul today) became the fourth and final capital.

We, however, needed gas. It was Friday, and apparently a fiesta day; the one-pump station on the outskirts of town in a very rural area was closed for the holiday.

We were really low on gas, and a crowd eventually surrounded us, all discussing our plight and what to do about it. Several men thought the owner of the station had gone to the cinema. Another man offered to fetch the station owner from his movie. A young boy, who said his name was Timo Chen, left and returned with a carefully balanced contraption hanging from a ring by three chains supporting a brass tray holding hot red tea in glasses for us. Meanwhile the other men went to the cinema as promised and did, indeed, return with the station owner, while we were calmly drinking hot clove/cinnamon tea (like drinking hot mouthwash).

Yes, we did get our gasoline, and off we went after many handshakes, back slaps, hugs and goodbyes.

What a wonderful scene of friendship and gentility, worthy of a film — or maybe mention in a book?

We arrived in Istanbul at about 2:00 am and found a really horrible flea-trap hotel in the old city by the port with the intention of finding something better first thing in the morning. Cheap? You bet it was (two rooms with bath for 10 lire each). But frugal though we were, *we still had principles.*

My first impression was a very dark city — no street lights or stop lights,, crazy traffic, pedestrians in dark clothing darting across the street in front of our car because no one stops or even slows down. Was I wrong? When I asked, because I saw no stoplights anywhere, I was told that, in the whole of Istanbul, there was only *one*. This was in 1957. Statistics claim the population grew tenfold between 1950 and 2000, so we saw it as a much smaller city than it is today. I returned to Istanbul several times on business during the sixties, when things seemed better — well, a *little* better. I enjoyed the food in Turkey. The Turks themselves were odiferous, but the raki (an anise-based alcoholic beverage) was great.

We got up early; moved to the somewhat better Hotel Londra and visited the Sultan Ahmed Mosque (Blue Mosque), Hagia Sophia (originally built as a Christian cathedral), the Topkapi Museum, and of course the Grand Bazaar for gift shopping and the ubiquitous puzzle ring. Legend has it that the ring was given as a wedding ring. If the wife took it off her finger to entertain a lover while her husband was away at war, the ring would fall apart, and she would not know how to put it together and back on her finger. Her husband would then know she had been unfaithful while he was away.

Now we had to think of getting back to Paris — back through Greece, back through Yugoslavia, and then we would probably go up through Austria and Switzerland. Our last night in Istanbul, we celebrated at the top of the Hilton Hotel overlooking the city and the Bosporus — *budget be damned!*

We made it to Thessaloniki the first day and spent time taking photos of mosques on the Turkish side of the border and exchanged currency at our hotel at an *unofficial* exchange rate. Unfortunately, we were given six 1,000 dinar notes, which were confiscated at the border because, being honest people, we declared them. In return, we received a voucher that we were to take to the bank in Belgrade *after sixty days* to get US dollars back. If they reimbursed at the official rate, we would come out ahead, but we weren't counting on that.

We had lunch in Skopje, and then the weather turned cold and foggy. It began to snow, which made the dirt roads to Belgrade even more treacherous. We couldn't find hotel accommodations, but one hotel manager directed us to a family who took us into their home for about $1.50 each. Very comfortable indeed. Very lovely people.

The next day we tried again to peddle our vouchers, and the story changed. Now we were told that *after sixty days*, we could change the vouchers for dinars (not US dollars) and that we could have spent the 1,000 dinar notes if we had simply smuggled them into the country. Sometimes you just can't win.

May 8 we bought salami sandwiches and left Belgrade, a very clean but stark city, lacking in warmth and with no vehicle traffic to speak of. We got on an auto route and proceeded to run out of gas, expecting to find a nonexistent gas station near Belgrade. (If you don't have cars, why would you need gas stations?)

I hitchhiked about ten miles carrying two 1-quart thermos bottles and a cognac bottle for gas (should I come across a gas station). When I found one, the nice gentleman loaned me a 5-liter jerry can so I didn't ruin my thermos bottles. It's not easy hitchhiking when there are essentially no cars on the road, but the bright side is that *everyone* will stop for a hitchhiker. It only took one; that's just the way these people were — *wonderful.*

North of Zagreb, we hit a chicken right in front of a group of soldiers. Needless to say, we kept moving but fully expected to be chased down and held for *chicken ransom.*

We stayed in Graz, Austria, for the night, had a wonderful breakfast (finally, cold milk), and headed for Vienna. This time, we hit a pheasant, which broke the glass in the outside mirror. I was not driving for either the chicken or the pheasant incidents, though I had backed into a pole and bent the rear bumper a bit earlier in the trip.

We made Vienna by noon, ate lunch, and drove out to the Vienna Woods and to the famous carnival with the giant Ferris wheel featured in the film *The Third Man.* Sure, of course we rode the Ferris wheel and looked for Harry Lime. (I heard that Yo wet herself in the house of horrors, but I can't confirm that.)

After lunch in Salzburg, we were on to Innsbruck. Now we were really in the beautiful, impressive Alps. We browsed, took photos in the old town, shopped, and drove toward the Grimsel Pass, which, we found, was already closed due to heavy snowfall; so we went by way of Zurich into Lichtenstein and Switzerland.

Then, it seems my co-pilot hit a motor scooter, but no serious damage resulted, just a scratch and a dent.

Because of the confusion, we arrived in Berne rather late. You must realize that we four companions plus baggage had been holed up in my magnificent powder blue Volkswagen for a month, and sometimes patience … well, you know how it is. This night, we witnessed a snit.

Her Highness was carrying on; nothing but the "Ritz" would do. It seems it was my turn to find lodgings that day. I tried several hotels to no avail, but the last concierge phoned a youth hostel and set it up for us for $.50 each. Hostels catered only to the "under twenty-five" backpackers and students, and it is a cooperative system; everyone as expected to help by sweeping floors or making beds up in the morning, which we were more than willing to do. We were desperate, and Her Highness was borderline hysterical by that time. We hadn't had dinner yet.

"Hostels won't allow you go out after 10 o'clock," "You can't smoke in a hostel," " I get sick if I don't eat!," " We'll have to sweep floors in the morning," " Let me out of this car at a decent hotel," and on and on from Her Highness.

Yo and I laughed about it.

The hostel did, in fact, allow us to go out after 10 pm but all we managed to scare up were ham sandwiches, beer, and tea; the Swiss close up shop early. We slept in a dormitory with fourteen (empty) beds. And, *yes,* we did sweep floors in the morning. And we had breakfast outside of Berne, a plate of ham and one hard-boiled egg each. Her Highness started up again, so we ordered an additional two fried eggs for her.

Did I mention that Her Highness absolutely freaked out in a thunderstorm? She explained that, when growing up, at the threat of a thunderstorm, her mother would close herself and the children in a closet. She instilled terror in those poor kids — traumatized for life.

And yes! We made it to Dijon by noon and Paris before dark. We dropped Yo off at her home and got Her Highness settled in … wherever.

The next important work in Paris was preparing our painting show,*Artistes Americains Fulbright*, June 4 through 28, 41 rue du Faubourg Saint-Honoré, sponsored by the Centre Cultural Américain and the Commission Franco- Américain d'Echange Universitaires. I entered "the big blue painting, the red painting, the brown painting, and the little green painting with lines."But now, more than sixty/seventy years later, I can't remember those works described in my diary. Nor do I have any idea where they ended up. So I must defer to the lady's remarks below. I sent invitations to many friends who came to the vernissage, including Mrs. Lee, Hollywood actor Mischa Auer, and Columbian ambassador to France (and briefly president of Columbia in 1979) Walter Guevara and his beautiful wife, Rosa Elena. And once again, the champagne flowed freely.

A charming, elderly French lady approached me and said that she liked my paintings the best—*"better than Picasso,"* she said. She awarded me first prize, bless her heart. And bless the champagne she must have consumed and what exquisite taste she had in art, *non?*

Darthea Speyer brought the director of the Chicago museum to the show. He also liked my paintings, but I suppose he said that to all the artists. After the vernissage, I went to Darthea's apartment with a gathering of artists and a *Life* magazine writer. The group split up for dinner. Darthea and I went to a tiny restaurant with sawdust on the floor and the menu on a blackboard in Montparnasse, and then the group regathered at Fred Thury's studio, where we were told to bring a bottle of something to drink and share, and a candle (because the studio had no electricity or working plumbing. It was to be torn down after he vacated it).

On June 9, I went to the Lorjou show under a tent on the Esplanade des Invalides near my apartment. Actually, it was an enormous, colorful frieze of brutal, often grotesque images of birds and humans. I was not familiar with his work until then, but I saw a large original Lorjou painting in the home of friends years later.

Job hunting had been promising; I was hired by Bodiansky to work on a competition for Cité de l'Enfant for about three weeks — afternoons only at 450 FF an hour, but it kept me in escargot for a while.

By July 1, we had vacated our apartment (within an apartment) and began our third and final big trip — Denmark, Sweden, Norway, and Finland, passing through Germany on the way. We went south to Bavaria as soon as we entered Germany to see King Ludwig of Bavaria's most famous dream castles. Neuschwanstein, above the city of Hohenschwangau - Disney's Sleeping Beauty Castle inspiration. It was entirely decorated with themes from Wagner operas. And Linderhof, the smallest of the three palaces built by King Ludwig II. It was easy to see why he was called the Fairy Tale King and, at the same time, *Mad King* Ludwig because of his extravagances. We spent the night in Munich and went to the American consulate for information on driving to Berlin. "We don't recommend it, but you are welcome to try." So what was the risk? Thirty years in a Stalag maybe? We decided to give it a try.

Heidelberg is a charming college town famous for Heidelberg University, the very baroque Old Town, Heidelberg Castle, and the Philosophers' Walk. We walked the Old Town area and had lunch at the Red Ox Pub, a popular, historical student hangout. Remember music from *The Student Prince*?

In Ulm, while having the car serviced, I had an electric gas gauge installed for $10. We had already run out of gas once in Yugoslavia because I'd forgotten I had already flipped over to the reserve tank. (Once was quite enough.) Ulm was known for having the church with the tallest steeple in the world (529.95 feet) until Gaudi's church in Barcelona. While often referred to as a "cathedral," the church in Ulm has never been the seat of a bishop. I was fascinated by the treatment of the spire. The stonework itself is very open; like lace or filigree. I have never seen stonework so light and airy. It was quite exquisite.

After a night in Braunschweig, we were determined to drive into Berlin, a distance of 110 kilometers at fifty kilometers per hour maximum speed through Soviet territory, but the paperwork necessary was confusing. "They" said we needed three things, but no one could explain what those three things were exactly. Finally we found out. We needed (1) visas, (2) road tax paid, and (3) a police stamp. Fine! *Done*! After much wasted time, we passed through Western control and were off to Berlin — driving very carefully. It was raining; the countryside was dull and flat with nothing to see but huge propaganda billboards with anti-capitalist messages.

We arrived okay but couldn't locate Centre Ville, so we just followed trolley tracks and traffic, figuring they should lead us somewhere. They did — right into *East* Berlin. *Hmm*, were we supposed to be here? We had not passed any Soviet control points, but we realized that traffic had reduced to nothing, and we were surrounded by many more war ruins. We carefully backtracked, asked directions to the American zone, and decided we had better check this out and be more careful. We finally found Centre Ville, the partially destroyed cathedral, and some new buildings by Le Corbusier, Walter Gropius, Oscar Niemeyer, and other architects who had contributed to the 1957 International Building Exposition. We found a wonderful pension a block away — large rooms; well furnished, with desks and easy chairs; and owned by a lovely couple with an adorable little white dog.

I forgot to mention that Yolanda couldn't accompany us on this, our third big trip, so it was just three of us — the lovebirds, which included Her Highness, and me and my beautiful powder blue Volkswagen. Her Highness had her own room; we, the guys, had the second room. Okay so far? It had been agreed by the lovebirds that any place we stayed for two or more nights, he got a night off (her idea) so the guys could go out together. When he explained this to me, I laughed out loud. "My friend, I know women, and I can guarantee you; it will *never* happen. Wait and see."

So, Berlin was to be the test.

Before dinner, she reiterated the deal she had agreed to. By the time dinner was over, and she realized that *he fully intended* to take his night off and go out on the town with me, she had her act all ready to go. It was tears; it was hysterics, it was ...well, you can imagine the rest. They disappeared into her room and were not seen again until morning. I went out walking alone.

July 9 we saw it all — the buildings of the Free University of Berlin, the Berlin Airlift Monument at Tempelhof Airfield, the Garden of Remembrance, and Stalin Allee or Karl-Marx-Allee (Moscow Modern architecture in the wedding cake style, covered with ceramic tiles, architecture that begins and ends with open space and ruins from the war, really monumental, grim, and unattractive. We saw Marienkirche, Unter den Linden (one of Europe's grand boulevards in the 1920s, as well as the cabaret, night club, and shopping boulevard, but then in 1957, we saw ruins on either side) and, of course, the famous Brandenburg Gate. The next day, we visited the 1957 Berlin Interbau (International Building Exposition).

On July 10, we visited a veritable smorgasbord of architectural fine dining, all in one location - mainly apartment buildings by the world's most prestigious architects; some still unfinished but open to the public nevertheless. A chairlift took us the length of the exposition — about two kilometers — and return. We drove to Hugh Stubbin's striking Haus der Kulturen der Welt (House of the World's Cultures), which was still under construction. *An unfortunate aside:* On May 21,

1980, the roof collapsed, killing one and injuring numerous people. I hate when that happens, but it was rebuilt in time for the 750th year anniversary of the founding of Berlin.

Contributing architects included Alvar Alto (Finnish), Le Corbusier (Swiss/French), Walter Gropius (German), Arne Jacobsen (Dane),and Oscar Niemeyer (Brazilian), to name a few of the better known among the many.

Two days later, we arrived at the Danish border, paid one month road tax, and waited a couple of hours for the ferry to take us over to Copenhagen, which is on an island. Unable to find lodging, we finally contacted a private home through a tourist office at the train station for $1 each per night—no running water (a pitcher and bowl by the bed) and beds hard as rocks.

The next morning, I began trying to contact Toby Faber, who was on vacation for two more days, toured the town all day, and planned to visit Tivoli Gardens that evening. Of course we saw the famous "mermaid on the rock" statue, which is much smaller than one expects—not very impressive really.

Tivoli was fun. With outdoor concerts and fireworks every night, it was a veritable fairyland of color, lights, and crazy rides. We drove out to the Deer Park, a forest park, home to hundreds of fallow and red deer, visited a modern Gothic church on the way and went back to Tivoli for the famous pantomime theater—one of Tivoli's landmarks and the only theater in the world where pantomime is *still* presented as an independent art from. We toured the fish market and the Tuborg beer factory. I'm not much of a beer drinker, but since the day was rainy and dreary anyway, why not?

We had a two and a half hour wait for a ferry over to Sweden, only making it to Gothenburg for the night. The second largest city in Sweden, Gothenburg was home to the University of Gothenburg and Chalmers University of Technology. We find that Swedish railroad stations have excellent, reasonably priced restaurants and an office for placing tourists in private homes; a practical alternative to hotels, which are scarce up there. The people were always friendly and charming, and they seemed to love Americans.

The next day we crossed into Norway at a beautiful natural gorge, on our way to Oslo. The scenery was so impressive we decided to buy sandwich makings and lunch by the side of the road. As soon as we arrived in Oslo, we stopped at a police station and located Jan, a Norwegian exchange student who spent a high school year with my family in Syracuse, New York. We drove out to his family's house. His parents were at their new summer house on the south shore, so Jan and his older brother cooked dinner for us.

Another night in a private home — we'd only had three baths since leaving Paris, and only two of those were with hot water. We were about due for another, and I'm sure you would have agreed.

We did the expected sightseeing, including the Viking ships and Kon-Tiki, the raft that crossed the Pacific Ocean in 1947 from South America to Polynesia in 101 days. It was an experiment to prove that it *could* have been done by South Americans in ancient times, using only available materials and ancient raft-building techniques. This gives support to the theory that Polynesia could have been originally settled by people from South America. We visited the folk museum of preserved houses and the Vigeland sculpture park.

Vigeland Park is a must-see in Oslo. It's the life's work of Gustav Vigeland, with over two hundred sculptures in granite, iron, and bronze, of people of all ages — fat, skinny, infants, children, old people, and older still — *and all naked*, doing all sorts of activities. Why naked? Vigeland wanted them to be timeless, and if they were clothed, they would be fixed in time; dated by their clothing. But the naked body is timeless. So ... makes sense to me. Of course we took silly photos, mixing ourselves in with the sculptures. We took showers in a public bathhouse for 1 krone. Now *that* was a krone well spent.

Next stop, Trondheim, about 350 kilometers on dirt roads that were very basic — in other words, *not good*. We were beginning to encounter patches of snow. The terrain was rocks, scrub growth, rushing creeks with rapids and not much else — what I call *desolate but beautiful*. We were crossing fjords (the long narrow inlets with steep sides gouged out by glacial erosion). And at 11:00pm, we could read a newspaper outdoors. Once again, we were staying in a private home with wonderful meals at wonderful prices. The exchange rate was 1 krone for $ 0.14, so our lodging was $1.10 and a full meal was$.85. If we cover 300 km the next day, we would cross the Arctic Circle. The roads were dirt but always well graded — no potholes or ruts — so we could make good time.

We climbed onto barren plateaus and then down through beautiful forests, along raging rivers and picturesque fishing villages with fish hanging on drying racks.

We crossed the Arctic Circle at about 9:00pm — still light as day and quite a lot of snow on the ground, but we were high on a plateau and the mosquitoes were intolerable. Apparently there was much logging activity, as we saw logs crashing down the raging rivers. We obtained our Polar Passports (a document for tourists crossing the Arctic circle for the first time.) and drove on to Bodø, arriving at midnight. Because it was daylight, children were playing outside, riding bicycles, and making noise as children do; it was weird. Again we were staying in a private home, hanging blankets over the window so we could sleep.

As a teenager, I'd loved the works of Edgar Allan Poe and had read every one. I first read about the existence of maelstroms in a Poe story, "A Descent into the Maelstrom." When I read that the strongest natural maelstrom on earth, the Saltstraumen, was located about twenty miles southeast of Bodø and remembering Poe's story, I said, *"Gotta do that. We must go there."* And we did; on July 20, 1957.

The strait at its narrowest is about 500 meters across. Water rushes through the channel four times a day, making navigation dangerous in the strait, so only a short time is available for large ships to pass. The impressive strength of water passing through is caused by the world's strongest tide, occurring in the same location during the new and full moon. A narrow channel two miles long connects the outer Saltfjord with its extension, the larger Skjerstadfjord, causing a colossal tide that, in turn, produces the Saltstraumen maelstrom. What a site — like a giant bathtub drain. As I stood there intrigued, *I could imagine a three-masted schooner caught in the maelstrom;, spinning faster and faster in ever-tightening circles; being sucked helplessly in toward the center, where it would be swallowed up to disappear forever - or maybe to be spit out somewhere on the other side of the earth.* Such is the imagination of a die-hard Edgar Allan Poe fan.

The next day we would have to backtrack about fifty kilometers to join up with the only road north to Narvik.

Before reaching Narvik, we had four fjords to cross by ferry, and these ferries had limited space for passenger cars. Buses took priority over passenger cars, and there seemed to be at least four buses of the Norge Line ahead of us at each fjord. Besides our group of passenger cars heading north, there could be other local cars entering the waiting line at any crossing, so it was up to us at each ferry landing to get off the boat and race to the next fjord ahead of the others. We hoped to be first passenger car in line for the next ferry. My underpowered but beautiful PBVW performed well in these veritable gymkhanas. I did know, however, that I had slow leaks in at least three tubeless tires, which required plugging as soon as possible, being that we were approaching the top of the world. And then what?

The scenery by now was spectacular — mountains of pure rock, scraped clean by the ice and snow and crystal clear water in the rivers, lakes, and fjords. We arrived in Narvik at

10:00pm, stayed with a family, and continued on toward the last fjord crossing before Tromso in the morning. At lunch, halfway between Narvik and Tromso, we had our first reindeer meat (that we knew of; sorry, Santa) called *dyresteak*. As the reindeer was a semi domesticated animal, the meat did not have a gamey flavor as one might expect. I was able to attend to my tire problems in this town, so now we were driving on three plugged tires, which added considerably to the intensity of this enterprise.

Not far out of town, we had our first encounter with Laplanders (or Lapps as they are referred to up there) — apparently a family in two teepees with many dogs running around. Her Highness was sulking for some reason only another woman could fathom, so she remained in the car, while we, the two guys, got out to see what wares the Lapps were selling. As usual, their typical footwear, hats, mittens, and reindeer antlers were spread out for us to see.

But first, who *are* these people called Laplanders? Let's try *Wikipedia*. "The Sami people (also Sámi or Saami, traditionally known in English as Lapps or Laplanders) are an indigenous Finno-Ugric people inhabiting the Arctic area of Sápmi, which today encompasses parts of far northern Norway, Sweden, Finland, and the Kola Peninsula of Russia. Some earlier anthropologists have suggested they might be of Asian and/or Siberian origin." So there you have it.

To us, they looked very *Siberian*, and they dressed in brightly colored clothing — very strong reds and blues. They were peddling handmade dolls, their characteristic footwear, headgear with earflaps, and the ubiquitous reindeer antlers. The Laplanders herd reindeer; or rather, I should, say they *follow* the reindeer herds rather than *control* them, though sometimes they try to keep them fenced in. As grazing animals, reindeer follow the food, and the Lapps follow the reindeer. That was why the teepees — easy to set up and take down, easy to pack up and go — were their homes of choice for the summer season. They built more permanent dwellings of sod for winter. This seemed similar to our American Plains Indians' nomadic lifestyle, moving their teepees while following the food-source herds across the land.

We didn't see any women or children, though they could have been staying in the tents. In Tromso, we could only find accommodations in a private home again. This was really an outpost town — wooden-framed houses in various colors, some well kept, while others virtually falling apart. We were on an island, so we had to take a short ferry ride to get there. We had difficulty finding food, probably because it was Sunday, so we settled for open-faced sandwiches and milk. Reindeer milk perhaps?

We went out to see the midnight sun. Okay, the sun descended *but didn't reach the horizon*, and then it started its climb back up in the sky. That meant it never got dark — in other words, night didn't fall. *Bummer!* (The midnight sun would be visible here until July 23.) It was 1:00am, and I was writing in my diary without a light on, and I could still hear children playing outside. Apparently, people slept whenever they felt like sleeping. Again we hung blankets over the windows to create our own personal darkness of night.

So far, we are averaging $6.30 a day apiece for expenses, including gas, food, and lodging — not bad.

On the second ferry, we met a curious American travelling alone — a regular Mr. Peepers (for readers who remember TV's *Mister Peepers*), clutching a Bible and asking many questions. He was touring Scandinavia for four months by bus, having left his motorcycle in Oslo. Every time we turned around, there he was — on a ferry, in a souvenir shop, in the town where we got the tire fixed — an apparition, all wrapped up in a huge, army surplus trench coat, easy to spot from a distance. We figured he would have liked to travel with us but wouldn't come out and ask, though he did ask, "If you saw me hitchhiking, would you pick me up?" He certainly wasn't destitute; he just needed companionship, and we were his target. He claimed he'd graduated from Carnegie Tech and expected to take classes in economics in London the following September. We agreed among ourselves that, if we took him on, *we would never get rid of him*. So we didn't – end of story.

Now on July 22, we were headed for the cutoff just before Hammerfest, which claimed to be the northernmost city in the world. Why, you may ask, were we doing this?(And you have every right to ask.)

I firmly believed that, as mountains were meant to be climbed and oceans were meant to be crossed, so Hammerfest was meant to be visited by my PBVW (powder blue Volkswagen). And it shall come to pass …well, *almost*. At the first ferry we approached, we were told it didn't take passenger cars, which cost us so much time we decided to only go as far as Alta that day. Remember, this was tricky country, all dirt roads, though they were well kept and well graded. And besides, it was *very* cold. We came to a more permanent Lapp village high on a mountaintop. The houses were made of sod instead of the teepees we were so familiar with. Obviously, winter was on the way. The mosquitoes were humongous, and they were after our foreign red blood; you could see it in their eyes and their demeanor. Apparently, as we were told, the mosquitoes followed the reindeer too; not just tourists. Now we were seeing women and children in typical colorful clothing, with a dominance of dark blue and bright red and lots of dogs milling around. Following on, we descended the mountain to sea level and found more Laplanders, this time with their skin-covered teepees instead of sod huts. We bought a great rack of reindeer antlers for about fifty cents, which we attached to the front bumper of the car (they wouldn't fit inside anyway) as our *rite of passage* for being way up here on top of the world where, in fact, we really had no business being. The antlers served as us shouting, "Look where *we've* been." This group of Lapps had an adorable, tiny baby just able to walk, who toddled out to greet us dressed in his red and blue finery. We took a family photo for them. They gave us an address of sorts, so we could send them a print.

Down at sea level, we were seeing more large racks of drying fish, which I assumed to be codfish — at least they *smelled* like codfish. To be honest, I really don't know what dried codfish is supposed to smell like, but I can guess. *Whew!* Yup, boy, *that's it right there!* That's the real stuff, all right.

We made Alta — a tiny outpost with small wooden houses spotted throughout the hillside. We stopped at the only guesthouse; had a superb smorgasbord with roast beef, ham, and all the works for under a dollar; and afterward we found lodging through the guesthouse. Again we were with a family, which was fine, but the toilet was in the basement — not so fine.

Something caught our attention; it must have been a game or contest of some sort. All through Norway, children wrote down license plate numbers they saw, even far out in the country. (What do I mean by "far out in the country? For hundreds of miles, we'd only been "far out in the country.") When they saw a car coming, they'd stop, throw down their reindeer or bicycle, pull out a pad and pencil, chase the car, and write down the plate number. When we arrived at the home where we were to stay at about midnight, sure enough, a young kid followed us into the yard and wrote down our number. I kept forgetting to ask anyone about it. Now it shall remain one of the great mysteries of life — *my* life that is, so I'm trying not to worry about it…but then again…

The next morning, after a big breakfast of tea and cake, we left Alta, climbed onto a high plateau, and came across a very large herd of reindeer grazing on the tundra. We chased them, trying to take pictures while being eaten alive by those monster mosquitoes. There were Laplanders among the reindeer, but we finally gave up. The reindeer were not interested in posing for some idiot foreigners in a powder blue Volkswagen, beautiful though it was, who seemed to be annoyed by a few mosquitoes.

So, now Hammerfest was a stone's throw away (50 kilometers) to the northwest. But there was only one road in — the same road out and right back to Alta. A quick evaluation reminded us that (1) we had no friends to visit or business in Hammerfest. (2) Mr. Peepers with his Bible (which was probably a *Holy* Bible, instead of the regular kind?) and his army surplus trench coat would probably be in Hammerfest *and he would find us*, (3) we would end up sleeping in some stranger's home, perhaps with the toilet on the *roof* this time, and (4) more kids would copy our license plate number. We could practically see Hammerfest from where we were. Was it worth doing Alta to Hammerfest (50 km) and back to Alta (50 km)? We were already over 1,200 miles above Oslo and over 500 miles above the Arctic Circle. Decision made, so we headed for the border with Finland. No more questions about that decision, *please*.

After crossing the border, we encountered more Laplanders and another huge herd of reindeer. While chasing reindeer through the thin trees and brush, we encountered remnants of World War II and the Lapland War — wooden grave markers topped by German helmets with still visible insignias; the remains of a tank; and assorted abandoned, rusting vehicles; apparently just left where they were stopped in battle. Apparently the local people respected the dead; didn't take obvious souvenirs. We certainly did the same. The most northern parts of Norway, Sweden, and Finland had suffered occupation, invasions, relocations, evacuations, and so on by the Germans. It was all very confusing; worthy of further study but far beyond our job description at that time. The mosquitoes were now so big and belligerent that the only solution was to walk *around* them.

We tried to find lodging in the first two towns in Finland but had no luck, so we pushed on into Rovaniemi — 420 miles today. By that time, it was 1:00 am and still daylight; it seemed we were just about right on the Arctic Circle, and the weather was quite pleasant for July 23. We tried three youth hostels (nothing available), before finally finding a hotel. But our room had twelve beds dormitory style. We found a great smorgasbord though—hot meatloaf, assorted cold cuts, various cheeses, and all the milk we could drink for about a dollar each.

We crossed into Sweden and drove down to Skelleftea, known for fishing and gold mining, where we spent the night, walked around town, and had dinner for sixty cents each. Scandinavia was easy traveling because the towns were small and there were no cathedrals, historical *must-see* attractions, or architectural wonders calling for our attention. Up north, we were attracted to the characteristic wood houses, often painted interesting bright, decorative colors; the fjords; the raging rivers; the scenery; and the fascinating Laplanders, reindeer, and mosquitoes—*can't ever forget those mosquitoes.*

Of course we could have continued down Finland by road to Helsinki, but that would have separated us from Sweden by the Gulf of Bothnia—a huge body of water that was really an extension of the Baltic Sea. But then we would have had to rejoin Sweden by ferryboat from Helsinki to Stockholm. That was about a sixteen-hour trip with a stop at Mariehamn Island, which would have seriously stretched our budget, since my powder blue Volkswagen would be a paying passenger on the ferry also. Time was not our problem; money was our problem.

The next day we drove to Sundsvall. We didn't get an early start and preferred to stop around 6:00 pm to facilitate finding lodging—preferably in private homes, since they were cheaper than hotels even though they add a two-krone service tax. And best of all, it allowed us to meet the local people. Stopping earlier also allowed time to dine at a reasonable hour. We, as usual, found a charming home with a delightful family and a cafeteria serving excellent food nearby. According to a map on the wall, we have been above *all* of Canada and up level with Baffin Island, Greenland, and northernmost Alaska. Tomorrow we'd head for Stockholm, about 250 kilometers by PBVW.

(Perhaps I should clear up any confusion about mileage on our adventurous trips. When I speak of miles driven in the PBVW, I speak in American miles because the car was purchased with American specifications, and the odometer registered miles instead of kilometers. When speaking about distances to travel, however, I speak in kilometers — as called out on maps, road signs, or native information. Sorry I didn't explain that earlier.)

For the first time since leaving Oslo, Norway, we were driving on paved roads again. *Whoopee!*

As a guess, that would be perhaps three thousand miles of *dirt*. You would expect the front of my car to be all pitted from the dirt and gravel, but no; in all those miles we seldom had vehicles in front of us kicking up stoes. That's why we could often cover so many miles in a day, even on unpaved roads.

Before starting out, the lovely lady gave us coffee and cake but wouldn't accept payment, so we thanked her profusely in writing in her guest book.

When people saw our German "Z" license plate, they were a bit hesitant, but once they found out we were American, their faces lit up with great smiles. (They were not well treated by the German invaders during the war.)

In Stockholm, we found a suitable home and a cafeteria and went sightseeing and shopping, planning to drive to Copenhagen the next day, July 29. Now I began to think about this return trip thing. When we backtracked, everything should appear different from when we passed the first time, right? I mean, we would see the fronts of buildings we'd seen the backs of the first time, and now we'd turned right where the last time we'd passed here we'd turned left. So it was a totally new perspective — like we weren't backtracking at all; it would be as if we were in a time warp, and my powder blue Volkswagen had turned into a reverse time machine. Or would it just be déjà vu *backward*. Wow! I must give this more thought when I have time — maybe when I got to Paris. Maybe it would be material for a Ph.D. dissertation, right? *Uh-huh. Sounds like a weiner.* (get it?)

We didn't have the usual wait for a ferry this time, so we arrived in Copenhagen by 4:00 pm I called Toby and Jytte Faber, and we arranged to have lunch together. Then, later, I went to their home for dinner, and we talked until 1:00 am. We talked of MIT, and I thanked him for his recommendation for my Fulbright Grant. Toby (1915–2010) gave me a copy of one of his books on Danish architecture.

The next day, I spent most of the day in Den Permanente, a museum-store of the best in Danish design — furniture, glassware, jewelry, ceramics, and stainless flatware. Located on a walking street, no cars allowed, it was enormous, it was beautiful, and it merited a lot of time for browsing. And it was all for sale.

Years later, on a business trip to Copenhagen, I returned to that store, where I met a charming FCA working there as a hostess, who later gave me a key to her home for all future business trips to Denmark.

From there I went to the Hans Christian Andersen Fairy Tale House — a guided tour of H.C. Andersen stories as "live" exhibits, his study, and even listened to a recording of him describing his life and travels. I didn't know what to expect, although it was highly recommended, but I was most impressed – what an interesting way to present a great author. When leaving Copenhagen for Hamburg, Germany, we stopped in Odense to see the actual house where Andersen was born and lived until about age fourteen, when the family moved to Copenhagen.

Driving around Hamburg, we saw the city hall; St. Nicholas (which at one time way back was the world's tallest building); and, of course, the famous Reeperbahn, Europe's largest red-light, nightclub, brothel, and strip club district (offering carefully controlled but totally legal activities). A literal meat market of human flesh, Reeperbahn was made famous by post-World War II US servicemen, who of course nicknamed it the *Raper*bahn. Pretty gruesome, but it was popular with tourists who felt they must see this terrible place. *Right!*

Probably the most popular and famous souvenir for American tourists was anything stamped with "Gute Fahrt" (meaning safe or good trip, even bon voyage). Little old American lady tourists in *tennybumper* walking shoes can't get enough of those key fobs to take home as *tee-hee* gifts

Then we continued on to Groningen, Holland, a college town because of the University of Groningen and the Hanze University of Applied Sciences. Groningen is a beautiful, well-laid out city with bicycle paths everywhere. At night, most buildings are illuminated, creating a very attractive, theatrical cityscape.

So, now we were dealing in guilders. Our room, with a complete Dutch (lots of cheeses) breakfast was 4.50 guilders ($1.00 equaled 3.83 NLG), about $1.20. Every once in a while on this trip, we would empty our pockets, count our money, and see if we thought we could make it back to Paris before going broke. My biggest concern was that I might be obliged to buy a tire or two due to slow leaks — certainly *not* in the budget.

I remembered back in my childhood, learning about Holland, specifically the word *zuiderzee*, which stuck in my mind, probably because it was fun to say. Also stuck in my memory were the obvious windmills and wooden shoes. And sure enough, we were able to see them all. Wooden shoes (sabots) insulate the feet from the cold, damp ground and, when worn with felt slipper inserts, are very practical. They were very common in rural France also and in every fish market. Volendam was a town where many older women still wore the traditional Volendam costume daily, which attracted tourists with cameras. The town, its harbor, the fishing boats, and the ladies in costume create a historical atmosphere of old Dutch paintings. There were about twenty windmills preserved and protected by UNESCO in Kinderdijk — probably the best place to see and photograph a concentration of windmills.

Amsterdam of course — how could we not go there? We stopped by Rembrandt House Museum out of respect for probably the most famous of all great masters. They say that Amsterdam has more canals than Venice, but who's counting? Nothing beats Venice for sheer beauty and romantic appeal. What a shame that one of the biggest tourist attractions of Amsterdam should be the red-light district, with the "ladies" posing in their picture windows.

August 2, we drove to Haarlem (tulip capital of the world) and Leiden, to visit the Leiden American Pilgrim Museum (Leiden was where the pilgrims departed from, to settle in New Amsterdam (the southern tip of Manhattan Island) and Massachusetts. Having been born in Albany New York, settled by the Dutch in 1614, I felt obligated to make an appearance in Leiden.

Now *DenHaag* (The Hague), where we dropped off Her Highness at friends. Then on to Delft, where we did a walk-around visit, followed by Rotterdam. What impressed me most in Rotterdam was the imposing bronze sculpture by Ossip Zadkine, representing Rotterdam with the heart torn out of its chest — the center of the city having been destroyed by bombings in World War II. What may seem at first like just another war memorial is so brutal and so strong that it perfectly expresses the feelings of the Dutch people. I was emotionally affected by it; that image has stayed with me for all these years.

Medieval Bruges was a treat in itself. And 1957 seemed to be a banner year — concerts, pageants, an exhibition of contemporary Flemish painting, carillon concerts, pageant of light and sound, and illuminations. And all were during April, May, June, July, and August. The Play of the Holy

Blood, an open-air pageant performed several times during the month of August, was only performed every five years; we just happened to be here for it without knowing in advance.

The play is performed in three acts — (1) religion, (2) history of Bruges, and (3) struggle of the people. Its cast of two thousand actors appear out of nowhere — in the streets and on the tower, from the top of which angels blow trumpets — all beautifully illuminated. Bruges may be called "the Venice of the north" because of its canals, but I don't think I would go quite *that* far. (I seem to always be defending Venice. And why not? Venice is unique; there is only one, and it is very special to me.)

Hilversum was important to my program because of one building, which I was anxious to see. Hilversum Town Hall, built in 1931, the year of my birth (along with the Empire State Building and Christ the Redeemer in Rio de Janeiro; just thought I'd throw those facts out there, not that I think they were built to honor my "coming," but then, who knows?) is an important example of modern architecture. The architect was Willem Dudock. This building is admired internationally and recognized as "one of the most influential buildings of its time," according to *Wikipedia*, and I certainly agree. After all, I'd come a long way to see it, hadn't I?

Brussels was to become a last stop before Paris, but we did the expected tourist things anyway. We visited La Grande Place and *Manneken Pis* (Little Boy Peeing), designed by Hiëronymus Duquesnoy the Elder (I love the name Hiëronymus, don't you?) and placed in 1618. Oh, and we ate French fries….*Stop!* Did you know the French did *not* invent French fries; it was those Belgians. (And the Belgians do need something else besides Mannequn Pis to brag about). Just so you know, and please remember *who* told you that; thank you very much.

We didn't want to arrive in Paris too late in the day because, come to think of it, *we had no place to stay.* We had given up our apartment on July first and stored our stuff wherever we could.

We were actually homeless at that point.

I came to the realization that, *okay*, I was coming "home." But home, to what exactly?

I had no home.

I had no job.

What did I have?

Well, I did feel that Paris was my home now, after a year of trying it on for size and finding that I liked it. One quick year had gone by so rapidly, and there was so much more to absorb. How could I possibly turn my back and leave it all behind, wondering what might have been for the rest of my life? I was in the process of making another big decision in my life—a decision that would be forever, I suppose. For some time on this, my third and final trip of the trilogy, I began to sense, without realizing it, some anxiety creeping in. There was something I had been avoiding; something I was not ready to face, and time was running out.

The Fulbright year was winding down, the monthly checks would stop coming, and my Fulbright friends and acquaintances were making their plans to return to the States, to new careers or jobs or advanced studies. But I… Had I finally and truly made *my* decision to stay in France, Paris to be exact? *It looked that way.*

High school friends were behind me. Hometown friends were behind me. College friends were behind me. Fulbright friends were dropping back behind me. They weren't disappearing; they were simply sliding down a long incline into the past, their voices and faces growing fainter. In retrospect, they seemed like butterflies, flitting in and out of my life. Some of the many girls who slid in and out of my life had by now become a kaleidoscope of names— Judy, Marcia,

Flo, Anna Lisa, Verna, Libby, Nancy, Elise, Ruth, Rondi, Gerda, Renette, Turid, Denise, Cynthia, Jeanine, Mary Alice. They were a mixture of curious, funny, intelligent, annoying, professional virgins, just what one would expect for the age group. And the guys: Garth, Windy, Dusty, Pete, Chick, Lenny, Jim, Thibault, Thierry, Bob, Dominique, Henri, Sandy, were pretty much the same mixture as the girls. They would soon join the others scattered around the world as memories. Most I would never see again. Some I might see from time to time. A few would communicate in writing, but not many. I had no illusions; I was pretty much on my own. So let's get on with it, since it is my life we're talking about here.

Now Paris friends were beginning to fill the space, like shoots breaking above ground — some to be cultivated, some to be weeded out, some to be loved and discarded, some to be consumed, some to be forgotten.

Here I am, eighty plus years later, remembering and writing about those days, and the same feelings return as if it were yesterday. But it is not yesterday; those days are gone. They slid down the same slope into the past that is my only hope now — *my memories.*

Once back in Paris, I spent most of my days chasing leads concerning room rentals, hunting for small apartments; and sleeping on friends' couches or on folding cots in a friend's hallway — a night at the Hotel Tour Eiffel and then another night at the Pavillon Hotel and then back to Jim's couch, and so on. It was a carousel of places and names swirling faster and faster in my mind. There were trips to check the American Embassy bulletin board, the Alliance Française, the American Express bulletin board, the American Students and Artists Club bulletin board, the Fulbright Commission, the Student Tourist Service (which found me a room in a student hotel for a dollar a night), and the *Paris Herald Tribune* — back and forth almost daily. I felt like I was chasing my tail.

An actual entry in my diary:

August 21, 1957.

Sat in a café. Moved back to the Pavillon Hotel. Ate at Self Service for 375 francs (about 85cents). My room is at the back of the hotel overlooking an alley. I can hear noise of toilets and a woman's constant hacking cough. Beginning to feel like a French clochard myself — ragged clothes, no home, no work, eating cheaply as possible. Such is the life of a starving painter. Please pass the absinthe.

I received a check from my car insurance company for almost fifty dollars, for one of our fender benders I guess, and a Fulbright monthly check (but those checks were about to stop coming). Yet how could I complain?

I was in Paris after all!

As is the norm in small, cheap Paris hotels, rooms were often rented by the hour during the day or night and the walls seemed thin; stifling heat, the windows open. I was often awakened by amorous activities of a couple — a woman in ecstasy next door, even to hearing the woman profusely thanking her partner for his service rendered. No wonder French men seem so emaciated while French women look so radiant and healthy. Must be the wine, I decided.

I was constantly chasing leads for work in small architect's ateliers:

"Non, il n'est pas la en ce moment."
"I might have work for you in two weeks."
"I've filled my quota of foreign people I can hire for now."
"Yes, I need help. Can you start tomorrow?"

That was what I wanted to hear, and it was beginning to happen. I was hired by Lagneau, Weill, and Dimitrijevic (Atalier LWD) for work on *charrette*, which lasted for some time.

Still, I continued my daily calls to the likes of Bruno Zevi, Louis Bonnin, Daniel Badoni and Pierre Dorlut, Pete Harnden, Pasquale Carbonara, Ernesto Rogers, Pierre Devenoy, Belgioso,

Dubuisson, Feyton, Gaston Jaubert, Lublin McGaughy, Jean Laruncet, Jean Monge, Wogensky, Peressuti, and Michele Ecochard (who, many years later, became a close friend and fellow sailplane pilot).With the French system of only hiring for preparing competitions, I was taking no chances. But I was probably driving them all crazy with my regular inquiries for work possibilities.

The folding cot turned into something more permanent when one of the three occupants of a large but very dingy apartment moved out, leaving space for me. It was a very chic street address, however. Avenue Montagne, address of several couture houses, but a fourth-floor walk-up at the back of the courtyard (*au fond de la cour*) and no heat. Splitting rent three ways was a great deal for me; this I could handle.

Pete, a fellow from Texas who was between years studying architecture, made the big mistake of coming to Europe *before* finishing his education. I say "big mistake" because, if you finish your education first and then you fall in love with Europe, fine, you can stay, look for work, and so on. But if you come before finishing, the pressure from family and friends is … Well, *just don't do it*. But Pete did.

Pete was sharing an apartment near the Place Blanche with a French painter, and on Sundays they would prepare beaucoup spaghetti; pass the word around the artist community; and serve spaghetti, baguettes, and cheap wine, charge a small sum in order to earn survival money. I heard about them, attended several such dinners, and enjoyed conversation much like the writers and painters did in the 1920s. And I got to know Pete and the group— all starving artists.

At the same time, Pete's French friend was performing a do-it-yourself knitting needle abortion on his live-in girlfriend, and it was not going well. Seems he had been grappling for the fetus for some time, getting it out in bits and pieces. Pete couldn't take the situation or stand her screaming any longer, so he moved out. Fortunately, for me, Pete had a line on a great place in St. Germain des Prés through a French friend.

Pete was being pressured by his father to "come home and finish your degree, or I'll…" As I said before, that is not a good situation. So Pete decided he'd better go home to Texas. But he turned the contact over to me. I contacted the owner. We set up a meeting, came to terms, and Jim and I moved into an eighteenth-century two-story house behind a wall, with a charming garden complete with a *pièce d'eau* and an adorable pergola — 4 rue de Verneuil. We had the entire ground floor. This included a kitchen, which was actually under the apartment building next door; bath; bedroom with a fireplace; living room with a fireplace; dining room; and storage room. The bedrooms upstairs were used by the children of the owner when they had classes at the Sorbonne and the owners when they came to Paris for a weekend.

We were in heaven — lots of space and a great location in the midst of my favorite art galleries. It was also right around the corner from the Hotel St. Thomas d'Aquin, which really defined the next few years of my social life.

Chapter 9

Le St. Thomas d'Aquin

Starting in late 1957, I was introduced to the piano bar in the St. Thomas d'Aquin, a small, intimate Left Bank hotel. It still exists today but has lost its Bohemian character of the postwar days. It is now simply a Left Bank tourist hotel, modernized to please the older American tourists who think it's still risqué to stay on the Left Bank — *oooh! Naughty, naughty.*

The *caveau* or cave, a vaulted stone basement, as is found holding up most Parisian buildings, was, according to many, one of, if not the first of many Parisian *caveaux* to be turned into avant-garde nightclubs, where many French singers performed. Juliette Greco and Stephane Golmann got their starts right here at the St. Thomas.

The infamous Mme. Blanc, a somewhat portly, middle-aged Basque lady, was the owner of the hotel when I first discovered the bar (where I spent the majority of my nights for several years). I simply became part of the furniture, occupying the same position nightly, though I did not drink. Mme. Blanc, in turn, changed my name from Charles to Carlos — the Basque, or Spanish, version of Charles.

Mme. Blanc did not own a car but used taxis, which were very reasonable in the mid-fifties and sixties. From time to time, she would ask me to drive her somewhere, which I was willing to do. But while I was driving, she would try her best to fellate me — something difficult for the average man to refuse. I knew, though, that, if I accepted her advances, her barmaid

Simone, my soon-to-be partner, would immediately know of it. And that I couldn't have. Mme. Blanc was long on warmth and friendship but perhaps a bit short on morals, which is why her husband sold the hotel from under her a few years later. To this day, many years later, the name *Carlos* sticks with me by many of my French friends. At one point, I actually lived in the hotel, but more about that later. A neighborhood bar in Paris in those days had no closing hour. It simply stayed open as long as there were patrons whiling away the hours of the night. Ah, so civilized!

The hostess and barmaid, Simone, with whom I could not converse as I did not yet speak French, decided from our first encounter to become, in her words, *mon ange gardien* — my guardian angel. I couldn't ask for anything better, since she was both beautiful and somewhat older — a true FCA or femme d'un certain âge. Why question a perfect arrangement? I was twenty- five; she was ... *perfect*.

At that point, I was sharing a fourth floor (really *fifth* floor to Americans) walk-up at the back of a courtyard *(au fond de la cour)* on Avenue Montaigne, in the 8th Arrondissement, on the Right Bank of the Seine. There was no heating in the apartment of course, but it had a very chic address nevertheless — just off the Champs-Élysées, with its fashion houses, boutiques, cafés, and theaters. Two days later, upon returning to the apartment, I found a box in front of my door, with a note from my *ange guardian*. Inside the box was a beautiful beige Cashmere sweater; my fate was sealed. That evening, I put on the sweater and headed to the St. Thomas for the evening. It was the beginning of a wonderful affair and a rapid course in the French language as taught on the pillow with a long-haired dictionary.

I had had a two-year language requirement in high school for my New York State Regents diploma, which required four years of science (general science, biology, chemistry, and physics); four years of math (algebra, geometry and solid geometry, trigonometry, and spherical trigonometry); four years of English; four years of social studies and two years of language — and passing state regents exams in all these subjects.

I'd chosen Latin for my language requirement. Why? Because my sister had chosen Latin before me, so I inherited her books. Why else? I had no idea that Paris would be my eventual objective, so taking French had never entered my mind. Years later, I realized that it was a good decision *not* to have taken French in a US high school or college *unless* the teacher was a native speaker from France.

When learning French, I carried a pocket-sized spiral notebook, in which I wrote words and phrases phonetically that I realized I was hearing over and over in everyday conversation, words from advertising signs on the Métro, words on walls and in newspapers. Then I would find out what they meant. It became a game, and things began to make sense, like pieces of a puzzle falling into place — until, finally, there it all was; it dropped into focus as if through the lens of a camera, spread out before me. The realization that I had mastered the most beautiful language in the world, a language that millions of people only dream about learning, and I had done it much as a child would do it — by absorption, like children do. *Sur le tas* as the French describe it. *Nope*. No regrets that I didn't study French in school. What I do regret, however, is that I didn't learn to *type* in high school. But no boys would ever have done that back in the forties. Typing was what secretaries do for us, right?

I avoided Americans on the street, in restaurants, and so on, especially when they tried, *loudly*, to speak French. Call me a snob, but I have such an abhorrence of French spoken with an American accent that I run from it and I made certain that I did not allow it in my speech. I'd much rather hear fingernails on a blackboard. But at the same time, nothing enchanted my ear so much as when a French FCA spoke English. Whatever accent I did have by then was taken by French people to be from, perhaps, the eastern part of the country but never a place outside of France and certainly not the United States of America. Wherever it was, they could not place it and could not believe it when I told them where I was from. I spoke the language. I was working within their economy, under their laws. I had become one of them and I was accepted as such.

Certainly, we can agree that the French people can be difficult. I dealt with them for twenty years — at work, on the street, in stores, in my building, and in my flying club. In fact, they became a part of my life… no actually, they *were* my life. We all had the same pleasures and we all had our problems.

So there I was, after living for a year on $155 per month. When the Fulbright year finished, I had no intention of returning to the United States. A new life was opening up before me like a yellow brick road During the day, I looked for work in small French architectural offices. In France, architectural projects were awarded through competitions. Interested Ateliers would enter these competitions and present a preliminary design solution in hopes of winning and being awarded the job. No money was paid for these preliminary competition designs, so small offices only carried skeleton crews, the owners, hiring draftsmen as needed to prepare proposals or when they won a competition and needed manpower to actually produce the job. I was ready to sign on for either stage as a *grouillot* (a lowly draftsman; perhaps a student - a slang term commonly heard in French architectural offices or around the Ecole des Beaux-Arts at that time).

I needed the income, the professional experience, and the French language. Every profession has a unique vocabulary; a vernacular of slang expressions which go in and out of favor and are often regional. I absorbed a French vernacular for architects, one for industrial designers and one for glider pilots... and one for love. There is undoubtedly one for neuro-surgeons.

The system worked. Off and on architectural work, playing guitar and singing in cafés evenings, and selling a painting from time to time at least put escargots on the table. But late nights were reserved for the bar at the St. Thomas d'Aquin.

On one occasion, Mme. Blanc, the owner of the hotel, requested my services for the afternoon. It seemed a young relative of an acquaintance had come to an untimely death under questionable circumstances. And because of her less than acceptable profession, she was not accorded the usual Catholic church funeral and cemetery burial with a grave marker.

I agreed to drive Mme. Blanc and a couple of apparent family members to an obscure cemetery in a remote *banlieue* on the northeast outskirts of Paris. It was a cold, bleak winter day, cloudy and dark, with a misty rain hanging in the air — not an honest rain that makes puddles in the streets, suggesting that umbrellas be raised.

I parked the car. We exited the vehicle, and the four of us began a slow slog up a hillside through the cemetery, dotted with a few leafless trees. There were no paths to follow and no one around other than our procession wending our way in and around what appeared to be recent unmarked graves. No headstones were present, just obvious mounds of freshly turned earth, occasionally capped by a small bouquet of field, or even plastic flowers. I thought that this was probably the pauper's section or a plot given over to victims of less than acceptable deaths or professions in the eyes of the church. But this kind of winter day created a gloomy atmosphere that I usually found rather beautiful, but seemed mournful this time because of the circumstances of our presence. My imagination began to create possible scenarios in my mind. There was no weeping or wailing, simply sadness, in keeping with the situation.

We gathered around one of these mounds, indicated by a probable gravedigger standing nearby leaning on his shovel. We ourselves were wearing heavy, nondescript clothing, creating a scene reminiscent of peasants in paintings by Jean-Francois Millet as we stood there with heads bowed. A fifth person, unknown to me but who once again pointed out what we all presumed by that time to be the correct grave, said a few words and trundled off. We backed away, turned around, and began making our way down the hill toward the car. Nothing was said. What was there to say anyway?

At the invitation of Mme. Blanc, we made our way to a nearby café for espresso coffee and cognac to ward off the chill in our bodies and in our hearts. I learned over the years that many gatherings in France end up in a café over an espresso and cognac or calvados.

Not much was said during the drive to drop off my passengers—all in all, a rather depressing day.

The St. Thomas bar attracted an eclectic clientele. The "at-*mos*-phere" (as Mistinguett pronounced it) was comfortably friendly—much like a living room with a bar, and a piano with pianist *Bob*, who played quietly all night, meticulously marking down in a small notebook absolutely every song he played. This was a legal way that the author of each song received a few centimes every time that song was performed anywhere in the country (*les droits d'auteur* - author's rights). A text book example of "trickle-down" economics?

The clientele, by frequenting the bar on a regular basis, tended to develop relationships, as one might expect, and discuss/argue over the day's world events; politics; books; and, of course, food. The French would often become more vocal over cuisine than over politics. One or two couples might dance languidly to the piano ballads as the night wore on. One night, a young handsome client crooned a few favorites. I had no idea who he was, but I loved the way he sang. I asked him if he ever recorded and he said, "oui," and wrote his name for me on a scrap of paper—not as an autograph, just as a friendly gesture, so I could look up his records.

Sacha Distell, the name he wrote on the scrap of paper (which I still have) I learned since, was a popular singer and cinema actor. I have had many contacts with French celebrities and entertainers and appreciate how the French people do not annoy and fawn over them on the street or in restaurants and cafés as Americans tend to do (more laissez-faire I guess).

One night I met an American lady, a perfect FCA. She was frustrated in a stale marriage with a grown (spoiled) daughter and a husband who planned to run for some political office in the United States. He knew his wife was in the market for an affair. His advice to her was probably, "Please don't embarrass me here locally. Go to Europe for a couple of months and get it out of your system." She came to Paris with her daughter, a recent college graduate, to travel Europe by car. Friends back home had suggested they stay at a Left Bank hotel, and so they did. I met them at the St. Thomas, where she confided her story to me. This was a perfect Mrs. Robinson situation for the cast of *The Graduate*. Yet the book wasn't written until 1963, and the movie didn't come out until much later; 1967 in fact. But here we were in 1959, living the story of Mrs. Robinson...almost.

No, I didn't do what you are thinking. But I can assure you, she did. She was attractive and the right age for my taste, but she was much too American, though she did find a willing French gentleman who frequented the St. Thomas bar. I heard later that her husband did not win the governorship anyway.

I met American expatriates in their early days at the St. Thomas, many of whom went on to greater things as actors, writers, foreign correspondents, and broadcasters.

The late Bill Kearns, a popular American character actor and writer, became a close friend, as did his wife, Norma, and their children. So too did Jacques Marin, a French actor friend of Bill's. Bill would bring a fresh turkey and sweet corn to my office every Thanksgiving. He and Norma had a charming country *chaumière* (thatch-roofed cottage) in Ecrignolles, Ecrosnes; scene of many weekend parties.

When I knew Jonathan Randal at the St. Thomas, he was a young foreign correspondent for *The New York Times* and

The Washington Post, who eventually moved on to covering wars and writing several significant books on the Middle East. He wrote on Lebanon (*The Tragedy of Lebanon*); Kurdistan (*After Such Knowledge, What Forgiveness? My Encounters with Kurdistan*); and *Osama* (*The Making of a Terrorist*). I still see him on TV from time to time. He would appear on television at each American presidential election, broadcasting from Harry's New York Bar in Paris. Jonathan continues to live in Paris as far as I know.

The late Patrick M. McGrady (1932–2003) was a regular patron and contemporary friend of John Randal's. McGrady was author of five books (his first, *The Youth Doctors*, which he was working on at that time, was published in1968. It sits on my bookshelf today). He was also the founder of CANHELP, a cancer treatment resource service. Conversation was always enlightening; continuing long into the night if not *through* the night.

When Princess Margaret made her decision *not* to marry Group Captain Peter Townsend, rather than be stripped of her royal privileges, Peter left England, traveled alone throughout Europe and South Africa in an old Land Rover, and stayed at the hotel St. Thomas d'Aquin. What an interesting crossing of paths. I did not know Peter then, but I met him years later, well after his marriage to a wonderful Belgian lady, Mary Luce. She worked with us at CEI as a PR consultant. She and Peter had a home, La Mare aux Oiseaux, in St. Léger-en-Yvelines, and a *pied-à-terre* in Paris. We corresponded throughout the late seventies, eighties, and nineties until Peter's death in 1995. RIP, Peter.

(While it is none of my business, I'm certain that a marriage to the princess would probably not have turned out to be a success for Peter; fairy tale romances seldom are. But while Mary Luce may have had a striking physical resemblance to the young Princess Margaret, she was an extraordinary person and a wonderful match for Peter.)

One night, in fact the day I returned to Paris from St. Tropez, in hobbled an old friend and regular, Totote. I say "hobbled" because Totote required two canes to help her get around. She was a character, a personality, and very popular with us at the St. Thomas. Totote was crowned with a head of orange hair and always wreaked of perfume. Whenever I saw Totote, my mind's eye saw a combination of Colette and Toulouse-Lautrec's *La Goulue* — and I mean that as a great compliment for a great personality.

Totote drove a small Renault 4CV (4-horse), with the suicide (forward- opening) front doors, which caused embarrassment to many female drivers in skirts when they pushed the front door open and swung their left leg out before thinking. But that actually afforded easier entrance and egress for Totote and her canes. The 4CV always reminds me of a little bulldog — low to the ground, tough, growling, and ready for a fight with its low stance and louvered rear-motor hood. I almost purchased one, but the *Dauphine* became available.

But Totote didn't arrive alone; she brought a visiting friend, Henriette, from Caracas, Venezuela. and Henriette …was …*superb*. I won't even try to describe her; it's a matter of taste anyway. An FCA to be sure and *elle avait du chien! Ah oui* in spades. (*avoir du chien* is an expression used to describe a woman who has *dog*, promises all at first sight, who exudes sexuality in a slightly naughty way. A sensuality that is just not available to all women; sorry to say.)

I had arrived that day from St. Tropez; deeply tanned, long hair, white trousers, the typical St. Tropez blue-and-white-striped fisherman's shirt, and espadrilles on my feet. It was late afternoon; time for the *apero* (short for l'aperitif). The bar was almost empty; quiet, sultry. I greeted Totote. She introduced me to Henriette. Our eyes met. Henriette returned a complicit regard, and the inevitable night began. It was obvious that she had come to Paris to have a good time, and I intended to do all in my power to help her accomplish that.

Can't help it — I'm just that way.

We chatted for a while, and then decided to retire to Totote's apartment, where champagne was promised. We folded ourselves into the 4CV, and off we went. I believe I heard Simone say, "Amusez vous," in a somewhat sarcastic tone of voice as we were going out the door.

But maybe not.

We made our way to the 18th arrondissement, where I was stunned to find that Totote lived at 13 rue des Amiraux, a building designed by the famous architect Henri Sauvage. (Let us not forget that I am, and remain, an architect by profession, so architecture is *always* foremost in my mind — even when women are involved.)

Sauvage's art nouveau style was described as "rational" and "hygienic," as expressed in the writings of Viollet-le-Duc, with the facade stepped back at each higher *étage*. The address also includes the Piscine Amiraux, a long, art deco indoor public swimming pool. The icing on the cake was that the outside of this block-long building is entirely covered with white, beveled, rectangular ceramic tiles, just like the Paris Métro. These tiles, today commercially known as "Metro Tiles," are popular and copied around the world. What a surprise. Even at night, I was amazed by the sight of an entirely tiled, startlingly white, very large building facade.

As we approached Totote's apartment, the odor of perfume was overpowering and would certainly impregnate my clothing and hair. I learned that Totote's quite famous business was the production of *essence*, from which perfume is made, and that her lab was just one floor below her apartment, which smelled like a very expensive whorehouse (so I've heard). Totote explained the order of strength. *Essence* is the strongest as one might expect and not applied to the body, *parfum* is next, and then *eau de parfum*, followed by *eau de toilette* and, finally, *eau de cologne* — the weakest and most diluted, so least expensive. The best buy for fragrance versus lasting power is eau de toilette.

We continued chatting and sipping champagne (Totote drank *only* champagne) until Totote retired and left Henriette and me to our devices, plus a frighteningly ferocious cat we couldn't make leave the room. We made the best of the rest of the night. Once satiated, I untangled myself from the clutches of Henriette's octopus-like arms and legs and made my way home by taxi. Luckily, the cat was not a participant. All in all, a positive architecturally and odiferous but educational experience — for Henriette as well, she murmured through half-closed eyes.

I had to burn my clothes.

It seemed that there was something of interest on a regular basis at the St. Thomas, from intellectual discussions to political arguments to whatever customers chose to discuss after a fine meal and a couple of cognacs.

A group of junior-year-abroad students from Yale came into the St. Thomas, asking for *Carlos*. Obviously someone who had frequented the bar had spread the word back in the United States to go there and find me, *Carlos* — that I would be there sitting at the left upon entering, by the lamp at the end of the bar. My job apparently was to give them pointers about social life in Paris apparently, which I didn't hesitate to do. They were practicing their French while holding prearranged jobs in banks as part of their year abroad experience. Being from Yale, you can imagine the family names — all well known, all extremely wealthy, but really nice guys. Many of them purchased Alfa Romeos and Jaguars to take back to New Haven, Connecticut, when the year abroad was over. One of them celebrated his twenty-first birthday in Paris. As birthday presents, he received a number of oil wells and $50,000 to throw a party for his friends. He bought a Jaguar, 140XK, white with red leather interior.

Another student was being driven crazy by his roommate, who was just realizing that he was gay, and he couldn't accept it; he was shattered by the realization; crying all the time and carrying on constantly. In those days, it was not as easy as it is today to accept what life has dealt. I often wonder how he finally resolved his inner conflicts.

This was a period when, along with the hippie subculture in the United States, drugs seemed to be an expanding problem according to what I was reading. Of course, *hash* was the drug of choice of the hippies (cheap and readily available), on their trek through Europe, North Africa, and the Middle East on their way to Katmandu (their Mecca). It was known as "the hashish trail," and it was not without danger as some hippies didn't hesitate to rob their brethren.

In my lifetime, I had never been exposed to drugs of any kind. In high school, smoking a Lucky Strike behind the gymnasium was a major crime, but nothing stronger ever appeared. Through my six years at MIT, the same thing was true; I never saw drugs, so I can't say with pride that I was exposed and tempted but refused to succumb. In the Sigma Chi house, drugs were never even a subject of conversation. In my twenty years in Paris (1956 to 1975), the same thing was true. I never knew anybody on drugs at work, socially or professionally, and I was never offered drugs at any social gathering or event.

Now that I lived so near the St. Thomas, Simone would stop by and cook dinner for me before starting her work around 9:00 pm Then when the bar closed, at anytime between 2:00 am and 6:30 am, why cross Paris by taxi to her place when I lived within walking distance? That certainly made sense to me.

Meilée, a top model with Givenchy, Dior, and Jacques Heim, frequented the St. Thomas. She and I became close friends, with no romantic inclinations. Meilée was in love with Gaby Albicocco (Jean Gabriel Albicocco, 1936– 2001), a French film director who used several of my paintings on the sets of his successful short films. Gaby, in the meantime, was obsessively in love with Marie Laforet, a popular *actrice* and singer, who he featured in a couple of his long-*métrage* films and eventually married. Marie Laforet also appeared in a 1960's film *Plein Soleil* (*Purple Noon* in the English release) with Alain Delon (along with my friend Bill Kearns) based on Patricia Highsmith's 1955 novel *The Talented Mr. Ripley*. In 1999, the same story was filmed by Hollywood with Matt Damon as *The Talented Mr. Ripley*.

The Girl With the Golden Eyes (1961), *Le Rat d'Amérique* (1963), and *Le Grand Meaulnes* (1966) were successful films directed by Gaby. But when he and Marie Laforet divorced, he gave up directing and concentrated on the behind-the-scenes, business part of filmmaking, eventually entering into a relationship with Gaumont Brazil and moving to Rio de Janeiro, where he lived until his death in 2001.

Many years later (1975) when I had moved to Brazil, I contacted Gaby in Rio, and did some graphic designs for his Ciné Club in the Meridian Hotel. I've since read that Gaby fell gravely ill and died destitute in Rio in 2001) RIP, Gaby

The Americans still had many troops stationed in and around Paris in 1956 and 1957, which meant PXs — a source for alcohol, mainly Scotch whiskey. Imported Scotch whiskey was highly taxed by the French government if purchased legally, but if it somehow snuck into my bedroom closet, Simone could transfer it into official French bottles and take it to the St. Thomas. So I found myself funneling black-market Scotch to the French customers at the St. Thomas.

Really?

Me?

That doesn't sound like a smart thing to be doing. Oh, *what the hell.*

And life continued at the St. Thomas by night, mainly by night — often *all* night.

About that time, Mme. Blanc's husband had had enough of her shenanigans. She was one Hot Mama, so he sold the hotel out from under her. One evening, we were introduced to the new owner — an adorable, petite French blond, probably in her late fifties (though I never asked and never knew her age throughout the years of our relationship), a perfect FCA by the name of Annie. She had a despicable, ex-French Foreign Legion husband,

Belgian by birth, who served in North Africa. He was too lazy to work, living off Annie like the leech that he was.

My goodness, I was smitten again by this petite, beautiful, non-English- speaking FCA.

Since I did not have a solid job and my love life was closing in on me, I decided to return to the United States, work in an architectural office for a few months, save some money, let the romances quiet down, and return to France by way of Austria. There, I would meet Annie for a month of *sports d'hiver*, skiing together at Obergurgl-Hochgurgl in the Austrian Tyrol. I drove my beloved PBVW to Le Havre and put it on a ship to New York, where I intended to use it during my temporary stay in the United States. When I went to the *aerogare* to take the bus to Orly Airport for my flight to New York, Simone and Annie, plus other friends, came to see me off. Annie knew about Simone, but Simone didn't know about Annie. "Oh, what a tangled web we weave when first we practice to deceive!" It worked for some time, but our sins always seem to catch up with us.

Annie wrote long, beautiful letters while I was in the United States for five months, keeping me up to date on what was going on at the St. Thomas. I sent hers to the very practical *Poste Restante*, where married lovers receive mail in France. I still have those wonderful letters. I maintain that French is the language of love, and my French lady friends have proven it to me over and over.

We had a wonderful month in the Austrian Tyrol, but finally it was time to return to Paris, find a job, and get serious with my professional life.

Annie and I took a night train from St. Anton together. At a brief whistle- stop in the middle of the night, I got off the train with my skis and baggage. I had no idea where I was. I saw no one else get off or on the train and saw no controller or other railroad personnel anywhere. Nor did I see a sign as to just where I had debarked. It was dark, and I saw no building or anything resembling a waiting room I could enter and wait. I was obviously somewhere in the middle of France, but I didn't know where or how far I was from Paris. Nor was I in any hurry to get there; I had a week to burn anyway before making my appearance.

Since there was only one track, I assumed that any train that came by would be headed to Paris, so I boarded the next train that came along and slowed down enough for me to sling my baggage and hop aboard. Paris had to be its destination since there was only one track. Sure enough, I did arrive in Paris several hours later as expected, and when I looked around, I realized that *our two trains had arrived in Paris at exactly the same time*, and only two platforms apart. When I realized my predicament, I simply stayed back hidden by my own train, peeking around the locomotive while watching Annie's friends greet her. After they all left the station, I left and hailed a cab to a nearby neighborhood hotel, always plentiful near railway stations in France. The French railway system is superb; trains arrive and leave on time. You can set your watch according to their schedule. That was an intentional decision after World War II. Priority was given to the rail system. Attention to the highway network came later.

My intention was to hide out for exactly one week so I could arrive "by surprise" on the following Sunday, as if arriving directly from New York. So I spent the week in the small hotel, reading, going to the cinema, and hoping to avoid running into acquaintances. I wanted to appear, as if by chance, at the St. Thomas exactly one week later. My baggage tags would be the same. Annie played her roll. "So happy to see you. Why don't you stay here at the hotel?" And I readily accepted. Of course I had given up the wonderful *hôtel particulier,* 4 rue de Verneuil when I returned to the States for those few months.

So I moved into one of the sixth floor walk-up *chambres de bonne* (maid's rooms) at the St. Thomas. These rooms, common to most Paris apartment buildings, were what we would call the garret or attic, meant for a maid to live in. Located under the Mansard roof, each room had a dormer window, which made these rooms, though small in size, very popular with students. Outside the dormer window was a tiny balcony just large enough for one person to throw a pillow and curl up outside, reading in the sunshine, or for flower boxes — but not room enough for both. Running water and toilet were located in the hall for everyone's use. At the St. Thomas, they were converted into tiny hotel rooms. I furnished mine with a low single bed, a square travertine coffee table, and a hanging lamp — all three of my design. I loved the view of Paris from that window, overlooking the landscape of Mansard roofs covered in slate or zinc panels and the forest of clay chimney pots that define the Paris skyline and are the subject of many paintings.

(A point of architectural interest: A Mansard roof slopes back from the cornice of the building facade in a double pitch so as not to be visible from the street below, thus allowing the builder to add another story to his building. The cornice ended stone construction. The Mansard roof from there on up was constructed of wood *charpente*.)

Meilée, who was now living at the hotel, had the chamber de bonne room next to mine, and Annie the one next to her. Meilée and I would often have after-dinner coffee in my room, made with my alcohol lamp-fired coffee maker and sweetened with condensed milk squeezed from a tube like toothpaste. She would confide her many feelings about her life and concerns about her career to me, much as to an older brother. Meilée was an extraordinarily beautiful young woman without a family; alone in the French world of high fashion. Gaby Albicocco would regularly tiptoe up to her room late at night. Meilée eventually met a violent death in a car crash with Jean, her fiancé at the time, on a beautiful Sunday afternoon returning to Paris from a weekend in the country, top down, rounding a bend much too fast. The convertible hit gravel and left the road, flipped over the guardrail, and landed upside down on them. Both Jean and Meilée were crushed under the car. May they both RIP.

Back at MIT in 1956, I had purchased two records by a French guitarist and singer who I loved to listen to, though I could not understand the poetry of his songs — only the sound of the language, the music, and the guitar. I'd wanted to learn to play the guitar. I had loved the sound of his singing, the melodies, and the *sound* of those words I couldn't understand.

One evening, I was describing this French singer to Annie and explained why I liked his music so much. She asked his name, and I said *Stephane Golmann.* She replied, "Oh, he's a good friend; I know him well. He lives in London now, but when he comes to Paris, he stays here in the hotel since he began singing in this *caveau*; one of the first after the war. "The next time he comes, I'll get you together."

Sure enough, it wasn't long before he showed up. We met, had dinner together, and retired to my tiny (but well-appointed) room for coffee and great conversation. He was without his guitar, so he played mine. By that time, I had memorized several of his songs and helped him remember the words to some that he said he hadn't sung in years. Stephane died in Canada in 1987. RIP ami The caveau of the St. Thomas was one of the early postwar nightclubs, which is why Stephane Golmann stayed at the St. Thomas when in Paris. It seems that he and Juliette Greco had performed at the caveau under the St. Thomas d'Aquin. These clubs featured a popular Bohemian atmosphere; La Danse Apache, a highly dramatic somewhat violent dance associated in popular Parisian street culture (prostitution, and pimps at the beginning of the 20th century); short, black, slit skirts, striped, loose, low-cut blouses and a kerchief tied tightly around the neck, berets, smoke-filled rooms Scoth whiskey and Absinth flowed freely. I, with Annie's approval, looked into reopening the caveau as a charming hotel basement bar, but building regulations had evolved, and we would have had to add an additional exit. As it was, the single stone stairway to the basement was through the back of the tiny telephone closet, so there was no way to add a second exit.

Work for me continued pretty much hit or miss. But I found enough, as I said before, to keep escargot on the table. And playing guitar and singing American folk music in cafés and at neighborhood bars at night continued the Bohemian lifestyle to which I had become accustomed.

Life was good. I was happy.

I feel today that I was fortunate to have lived the final days of Paris's extraordinary post-World War II period, known as the Golden Years (1945 to 1975.) *Yes*, there was turmoil. *Yes*, there were problems. It was not a perfect time. France was struggling to get up off her knees, battered from the war itself. The Algerian strife, unrest in the African colonies and the closing down of an empire as countries took independence while stumbling into a different world with new problems lurking in the shadows. But it was still a happy, prosperous, and exciting time.

And I lived it.

I felt a serious change after 1968; problems became ultra-international in nature, probably because television, and eventually the internet and now social media, broadcast what was happening to the whole world in real time. Students are usually out in front of such turmoil — 1968 being a good example. Students at the Sorbonne knew what students at Berkeley were up to the very same day it happened.

I feel fortunate that I was not in the United States during those tumultuous times. I would never have been a part of the counter culture. I could never have been a *hippie* or a *yuppie*. I would have steered clear of such manifestations as Woodstock, the drug culture and their trek to Katmandu.

Those unwashed girls with the filthy, stringy hair chanting "Hare Krishna" were a total turnoff. I've watched films of the "great" Woodstock weekend and cannot believe that it has come to be considered one of the important cultural happenings of the century. Sliding around in the mud, listening to what I considered terrible music badly performed by drugged-out performers is not my idea of fun. Just the other night, NPR rebroadcast the entire Woodstock film. Once again, I forced myself to watch it. I saw Jimmie Hendrix whaling away playing non-music on his guitar to an empty field (because he didn't get there on time), and Janice Joplin screaming at the top of her drugged-out lungs is not my idea of music — it wasn't then and it isn't now. Of course, most of the audience was high the entire weekend anyway. They say, "Ya hadda be there." Well, I'm thankful I was not.

I also believe that this period was when the hippies turned left politically, though they were already on their way, what with their communal lifestyle, socialistic leanings, and so on. I witnessed a perfectly normal family member (same age and family background as mine, studied architecture as I had, and also a painter with whom I painted for a couple of years in Paris) return to the United States, get a teaching job in the art department at Wisconsin State University, Whitewater, and succumb to radicalization by the left — as thorough as that of ISIS and BLM working on young minds today. Brainwashing is a science; we see it every day with religion and accept it as okay. That family member is now a retired Marxist professor in a small liberal arts school in the Midwest, with a couple of marriages and three kids under his belt.

Many years later, while on a business trip to the United States, I visited him for a couple of days in New York City. He took me to a favorite hangout bar (his New York version of my St. Thomas perhaps?), where we sat talking over old times and saying hi to passing acquaintances of his, as one does in a neighborhood bar. I realized that I was not comfortable; I was in a very strange place. This was not my *milieu*; these were not my people. Yet I was born and raised a few hundred miles up the Hudson River. Had I changed that much?

Why was I so comfortable in Paris and so uncomfortable there in New York City? They say one can never go back. Maybe it's true; I couldn't image living in Manhattan or in my old hometown. This gave me much to think about in evaluating my situation. Could a city have this effect on a person? Paris had become like a female acquaintance, wheedling her way into my heart, into my brain, into my very being. And I was not only allowing it to happen, *I was enjoying every minute of it.*

Years later, I realized and understood that I had lived the turbulent Vietnam era as seen *not* through American eyes, but, through French eyes. I read the *Le Figaro, Le Monde,* and *France Soir* newspapers, (with the occasional *International Herald Tribune* thrown in but mostly for the Art Buchwald articles of that time). I read *L'Express* magazine and saw the evening news on French television. I listened to public discussion in cafés and restaurants. I was not affected by it as was America; I observed it from afar with the French population. My concern was the war at hand — the Algerian War, the *plastique* explosions I could hear at night, the *blessés de guerre* I could see on the streets and the specially marked seats for them on the Métro. I worked with designers returning from Algeria when the war ended, often suffering with amoebic dysentery from the drinking water or eating water-based popsicles in the suffocating heat of the North African desert climate. I lived the return of Charles de Gaulle to power and the independence of many West African countries as a Frenchman – not as an American. I was a good example of total assimilation.

Even now, so many years later, I can reminisce about Paris, about curiosities of French life in the fifties and sixties as if lying passively beside Paris *herself* and reminiscing, *as lovers do.*

Chapter 10

Paris, Comme Je t'Aime

(Paris, How I Love Thee)

Note: I consider the following to be a private conversation — musings if you will — between me and Paris. She is a city I consider to be of the feminine gender (though it is a masculine word) a city able to give love, and a city able to receive love, just as a woman in real life. She is as capable of pleasing me as she is of exasperating me; and she often did both, sometimes in the same day. She's seductive, sensual to her core, but capricious, oh yes; and what a temper. So while I have a few words with her, you are welcome to listen in on our conversation, which, I admit, is a bit one-sided. We met for the first time, as you the reader, knows by now, in 1956, and it was love at first sight — for me anyway. I'm speaking about the city itself, almost in spite of the inhabitants, but that doesn't make sense, does it? She probably doesn't know I existed in her life for the twenty years I lived with her, but I have never forgotten her; nor will I ever forget her.

You, *my love*, have had thousands of suitors over several hundred years — about nine hundred years I believe — and I accept that. To be sure, you were much older, gray with the smoke and soot of the ages, but that is exactly what I like in a city (and in a woman). However, I don't expect you to understand. You have lived a hard life, suffered revolutions, wars, and the expected wear and tear of years of abuse at the hands of men who mistreated you and women who took advantage of your charms. You too have the wrinkles of maybe too much experience, but they actually reinforce your attractiveness to me. The Industrial Revolution, with its coal and wood fires, affected your facades just as living in a smoker's house today affects the furnishings, as well as the inhabitants.

It seems as if, every few years, something troubling occurred that seemed abusive at the time. But eventually we had to accept it—as when a lady changes her hairstyle or has one of those unfortunate minor surgical procedures to subtract a few years from her profile while destroying her facial expressions and speech with puffy Botox lips.

Remember when that old curmudgeon Napoleon III commissioned George Hausmann to perform major surgery on you around 1853? I was not with you then, of course. But I understand that many old medieval neighborhoods were destroyed to make way for wide avenues, parks, and open squares — the excuse being that they were overcrowded and disease ridden. But still there was fierce opposition to this undertaking. To be sure, in the cholera epidemics of 1832 and 1848, many people died, so we must agree that something to alleviate the overcrowding and discontent was needed. In those days it was about horse carts on very narrow streets, not cars, busses, delivery trucks, and motorized bicycles. Of course, this many years later, we can appreciate that it certainly did improve circulation through the city, and the parks and fountains are beautiful today. But not all so-called improvements in later years, fared so well in my opinion.

The destruction of a charming neighborhood in Montparnasse to make way for the terribly unattractive Tour Montparnasse and its surrounding sad commercial shopping area was a total disappointment for me. I spent many a night strolling that old neighborhood in the wee hours of the morning. I would stop in at the Monocle, a smoke-filled lesbian bar frequented by strangely dressed men and women of all ages, dancing to an all-over-sixty ladies band dressed in wrinkled, ill-fitting men's tuxedos that hadn't seen a hot flat iron in many a season — a very turn-of-the-century atmosphere. The clientele was so varied it was impossible to determine who was what and for whom. Henri de Toulouse-Lautrec would have felt quite at home and been inspired to paint what he saw there through the acrid smoke of Gitanes cigarettes.

There were just enough ladies of the night at the corner café to complete the charm. Invariably, the corner ladies seemed to each have a child being cared for by the grandmother or aunt in a small town far from Paris. When one frequents a *quartier* in Paris, people on the street address each other and pass the time of day …or night.

I miss that, don't you?

You had it all, my dear. The passing years are seldom to our advantage, but you have held up well. Certainly when the Basilique du Sacré-Coeur was foisted upon you, that Romano-Byzantine basilica perched on the highest point in Paris, was mired in much controversy as to exactly what historical group or event it represented. And the Tour Eiffel? A wrought iron tower built specifically for the 1889 World's Fair was highly controversial at the time, since it towered above Notre Dame de Paris, the Panthéon, and other high structures that many felt should be held in higher esteem. Hector Guimard's art nouveaux metro entrances were derided by the public even for their green color. But now we love them, don't we?

Interesting to see, *my love*, how these warts of old have become your most valued assets (except for that horrible Tour Montparnasse, which I feel simply destroyed a wonderful neighborhood). While it hasn't been easy for you, you are a survivor, my adored one, and always will be. I hate to even mention La Defense; the western anchor of the majestic axis; Place de la Concorde – Arc de Triomphe – La Grande Arche de la Defense. Maybe, like the others, time will eventually make it right, but certainly not in my time.

Scootch over closer to me, *mon troignon*. C'est ça, *mon amour*.

I was used to a gray Paris. To me you were so beautiful in winter, when the days were short and it so often drizzled and dripped under clouds hanging so low that the top of the Tour Eiffel was swallowed up by them; I loved that atmosphere it created. If you remember, *love*. I never complained about the weather.

We were already lovers when Charles de Gaulle came back to power. I no longer lay in bed at night, hearing the *plastique* explosives going off in the distance. The Algerian war ended, the West African colonies took their independence, and de Gaulle decided that you were in need of a face-lift. I questioned it at the time, as did many citizens. His minister of culture, André Malraux, began a program of cleaning the facades of historic buildings and monuments in the 1960s, by light sand blasting, and all property owners were obliged to follow suit. What an undertaking... and what complaining.

So for years, we walked under scaffolding on gritty sidewalks covered with sand, but *voilà*! You, my love, were gradually transformed into a radiant, warm, natural beige color—the true color of your original naked self. It took a long time, but it was certainly worth it; and I'm certain you were proud, as any woman would be, of your rejuvenation.

My *envie de toi* increased, if that was even possible.

We had some fun times, didn't we? It seemed that you never slept. So many times you kept me out until dawn, knowing that I had to work the next day, and you knew very well that I hated going to bed when the sun was already up. But how you loved the night. It was at night that you introduced me to the most interesting people in the most unexpected places.

Remember the night you introduced me to a very attractive FCA in a Right Bank café? After a couple of hours of conversation she said, after writing something on a piece of paper.

"I will leave my door ajar for you if you choose to come to me tonight... at any hour. Here is my address and an explanation of how to navigate the complicated double staircase inside the *portail* and the *porte cochère* where I live."

That was certainly one of the most erotic, exciting invitations ever. She obviously wanted to talk more.

And yes, I was able to keep the appointment.

Your streets are narrow, and the street sweepers with their brooms made of long, bundled tree branches, couldn't clean the gutters properly if cars were parked close to the curb. On narrow streets, such as where I lived in Saint- Germain-des-Prés, parking was only allowed on one side of the street. Then, it was decreed that the parking side of the street would change at 7:00pm every evening (odd-even, odd-even).

I remember so well the nightly scene. At about 6:55pm, each *riverain* sat in his car, motor revving, waiting for the stroke of 7:00pm, at which moment, every driver tried to jockey his car into a space directly across the street from where he was just parked. It sounded like the start of the 24 Hours of Le Mans race — *shear madness*, and it happened every night. If you forgot to be there at the ready, and it happened often, your car would be the only car on the *wrong* side of the street, forming a chicane with those cars correctly parked. Awkward to say the least, but it was a game that had to be played. Right, my love?

Parking meters were out of the question in Paris. Eye sores on your quaint streets and beautiful boulevards? Certainly not! The next idea was for every vehicle to carry its own parking meter. It was a simple but ingenious solution. It was made of cardboard — and it worked.

These cardboard devices were made available at stationary stores at free of charge. They incorporated a revolving disk printed with hours and minutes, which would appear in a cut-out window. You parked your car, set your time of arrival, placed the device in the windshield so it could be seen from outside, and locked your car. The controller could then see if you were overstaying whatever the time limit was for the area you were in. A simple chalk mark on a front tire was a giveaway that you had changed your disk but not moved your car. You have to give them credit for such a simple solution to a serious public problem, *n'est-ce-pas, cherie?*

Another logical solution to a universal problem was developed in 1830. The *vespasiennes* (more vulgarly called *pissotière or pissoir*) came to be. At one time, back in the 1930s I've read, there were over 1,200 of these freestanding urinals throughout Paris — in parks, on street corners, on sidewalks around town. Men could simply step behind the knee-to-shoulder screen and go, without interrupting his conversation with a companion — male or female. I chuckled to read a *"Defense d'Afficher"* sign on each one (meaning essentially "Post No Bills") being ignored by posters stuck all over, advertising *PUR-O-DOR, Suze* or *Absinthe.* Granted they were somewhat odiferous and women hated them — jealousy I guess. (What about us? they cried.) The ladies won out, and slowly the pissoirs disappeared from the streets of Paris.

What a shame.

Remember the many afternoons we strolled the Marais, gazing through the *porte cochères* of the grand eighteenth-century *hôtel particuliers,* hidden within — like the one we lived in at 4 rue de Verneuil, where Simone prepared dinner before going to work at the St. Thomas and where we had those wonderful garden parties. Oh what memories, *mon amour.* Can it really be so long ago?

I can already sense the end of *my* time; just around the next corner. Yet your life will go on for hundreds of years, attracting the adoration of many lovers to come. It hardly seems fair somehow.

On our many strolls, we would sometimes end up in the Place des Vosges or on the Ile de la Cité or Père Lachaise cemetery. There we visited the graves of Balzac, Chopin, the Hugo family, Modigliani, Delacroix, Proust, Corot, Yves Montand, Simone Signoret, and eventually Edith Piaf; the mass grave of the147 insurgents of the Paris Commune's final stand in 1871; and graves of members of the Résistance.

I could only imagine how it was one hundred years ago. You were already there, watching the life around you — the merchants, the children running and playing, or the coal deliveries in burlap bags carried to the upper floors on the backs of the *charbonnier*, as it is still done today. Deliveries often blocked the narrow streets, causing much yelling and loud discussion from the vehicles trying to get through to make their deliveries and be on their way. Of course, that is still true today; and it's not about to change. In 1956, Citroen 11CVs and 15CVs were still on showroom floors, beside the ultra sexy Citroen DS, followed by the ID, being introduced. Those magnificent old *onze* and *quinze CVs* were the gangster getaway cars of every French film noir, with the suicide doors flying open and tommy guns blazing. We used them in the 1960s to pull trailers carrying disassembled sailplanes in our flying club. Used car lots and junkyards were full of them, so parts were easy to find. They were hard to drive, but they certainly hugged the road on curves and were great for towing trailers. It required a very strong woman to dominate one, but I knew a few who could.

I discovered French cuisine with your help and soon decided that this was the way God meant for humans to eat; correct, *mon chou?* And you taught me how to dine wisely, frequenting the myriad small, neighborhood places along with the student restaurants. All restaurants posted illuminated menus, either on a freestanding pedestal outside the door or hung in the window. These menus, were ingeniously created each day. Hand written on a smoothed modeling clay surface with a stylus, after which purple ink was applied with a roller. The ink pooled in the scratched writing which was then pressed onto a sheet of paper (much the same process as etchings on copper). Easy, quick and since only a few were needed each day for the restaurant, cost very little. But they all, without fail, had two dishes at the top of the *entrée* (after the soup; before the meat) list — *potage du jour* and *oeufs dur mayonnaise.* Both became favorites of mine. If they cost thirty centimes for the potage and/or fifty centimes for the hard-boiled egg floating on a bed of lettuce, I didn't have to look further, because I knew that all the other prices for the entrées and desserts would be within my budget. In my twenty years in France, I don't ever remember having a disappointing meal — *ever*.

In order for struggling students to attend museums, theater, and other cultural events, an office in the Sorbonne gave out free tickets to registered students for many cultural locations and events. Very inexpensive student restaurants serving excellent food were located around the Latin Quarter, open for lunch and dinner.

Tiny night clubs around Montparnasse, the artistic center for painters, writers, and art schools (like the Académie de la Grande Chaumière) offered free entry for registered students, but we had to arrive when the boite opened for the evening and stay throughout the evening. For that, each person received a half bottle of champagne. Why such a good deal? The main door into these small clubs opened directly off the sidewalk. Night strollers don't walk into empty nightclubs. They want to *see activity* — patrons sitting at tables enjoying themselves before the floor show started — a job fulfilled by the students, *decoys* as it were. The students themselves didn't have money to spend in nightclubs, so everybody profited. *Genial!* As Fulbright recipients, we were enrolled in an institution of some kind (in my case, l'Institut d'Urbanisme de Paris), so we would qualify for these student benefits, though we were not expected to actually attend classes.

Many French students lived in the small student walk-up hotels that were found throughout the Latin Quarter surrounding the Sorbonne. Lodging was incredibly inexpensive, but bathrooms and running water were down the hallway, if they were even available on the same floor as the room. All French buildings had *minuteries* (timers) to avoid wasting electricity. It was common for the lights to go out while we were halfway up a curved flight of stairs, leaving us in total darkness until the button on the next landing was pushed and the lights came on again — but just for a few minutes.

And the jokes you used to play on me, *trésor*. Like the ubiquitous *chauffe- eau* (water heater); an ingenious device to be sure, but they were always frightening and seemed dangerous to the uninitiated stranger, especially the one that almost beheaded me. It was in our Ave. Montaigne apartment, remember?

A chauffe-eau was a metal box hung on the wall in the bathroom, often right above the sink, whose purpose was to supply hot water on demand. It used gas as its "explosive." But let me explain. The metal box in question, about eighteen inches high by fourteen inches wide and perhaps six inches deep, incorporated a tubular copper coil through which cold water ran with the hopes of being heated. Below that was a gas burner with a pilot light, which most people only lit with a match when they wanted hot water. The French are a frugal lot, and the pilot light was certainly not going to burn 24- 7 wasting valuable gas. If the pilot light was lit, and you turned on the water, a very impressive *whoosh* was produced when the big gas burner came to life below the copper coil.

The water, which I had turned on hoping that hot water would come out of the faucet, was necessary to continue the heating process. If I turned off the water, the gas stopped flowing, and so ended my hot water flow — and my warm bath. The door on the front of this box was equipped with a rather large porcelain knob since, to light the pilot light, the door had to be opened for access.

So, I made the proper moves, turned on the water, and waited for the *whoosh* ...and waited ...and waited. Fight or flight? *Fight* — go forward and try to turn off the water, which would turn off the gas, or *flight* — back away before the impending *boom.*

Too late.

The sides of the metal box bulged outward from the blast, and the door swung open 180 degrees with such force that the porcelain knob buried itself in the wall.

Oh how you laughed, my love, *but that could have been my head!*

I loved the greetings each morning when I went to the *boulangerie* to buy fresh, warm bread just out of the oven — the *"sieur dame"* and the *"merçi m'sieur"* at the *fromagerie,* the *laiterie,* and the *charcuterie* when buying a slice of *paté de campagne* or *mousse de canard* for breakfast. Butter was cut from a large mound of freshly churned butter using a home-made, thin wire device with short wooden dowels at each end as handles.

I loved to order a strong espresso café at the counter by just using a simple hand gesture (the twist of a clenched fist) familiar to all French *garçons.*

I loved to see the quality of books people read on the bus, the Métro, and even on the beach.

I loved to see groups of young children listening attentively to their guide or teacher explaining works on a museum tour.

I loved the characteristic sound of the multifold window shutters being closed at sundown or the screech of the knife sharpener as he pedaled his sharpener through the streets, signaling his presence by applying a piece of steel to his sharpening wheel — a piercing noise that carried for blocks. The ladies gathered up their dull kitchen knives and descended the many flights of stairs to join him on the street, where he proceeded to have his way with their knives.

I loved to overhear the conversations of those having their morning *café au lait, tartine beurrée,* and shot of calvados at the *comptoir.*

When we strolled around your wonderful city, every detail jumped into focus and became important to me; things that ordinarily went unnoticed, now stood out. Like the rolled-up pieces of burlap in the gutter, used to direct the flow of water to the left or to the right by the man with the broom made out of a bundle of tree branches. It is pure Parisian charm. *But I wondered,* does he make his own brooms? Does someone make them for all *balayeurs*? in a factory somewhere? Maybe that's what I'll do in my hereafter, like a hobby — tie brooms for the street sweepers. After the novelty of such things wears off, they become commonplace and tend to go unnoticed - but not to me.

The water in the streets runs like blood in your veins, *my dear* — or maybe more like tears, shed for the injustices you see every day.

So you see, my *cherie*, you will be here forever, *though I will not.*

For *you* are eternal… *but I am not.*

Take heed, my love, and do take care.

Moi

Chapter 11

The Libertine Life

I had the opportunity, while living in Paris, to make the acquaintance of several very interesting ladies of my favorite age group, who knew of worldly, high-quality activities and where to find them. The French are expert at this sort of thing—eroticism coupled with their laissez-faire attitude seems to be in their blood. Though I have read that such things do, in fact, exist in the United States, I personally would shy away from involvement. I just feel that the American version would be tawdry by definition; probably because of our stifling Puritan attitude and history towards sex in general. I don't feel that our recent so called "sexual revolution" improved the situation. Young people turned sex into a sport while the older ones said, *"What just happened?"* and *"Why wasn't I included?"* Our basic Puritan mores twist simple pleasures into "flirts with the devil." Why is it that men today seem to treat women badly, according to the scandals I see and read about? I don't get it.

The oldest *maison de tolerance* (not to be confused with bordello or other forms of prostitution) I know of was established in the 1930s, in a small *banlieu* town southwest of Paris along the rue de Versailles. A *maison de tolerance* is simply a place where "everything is possible, but nothing is obligatory."

The rue de Versailles passes through several charming small towns on its way from Paris to Versailles—Meudon Val Fleury, Villed'Avray, Chaville, Viroflay, and Sèvres. I happened to live in Meudon Val Fleury in the early seventies, and the *maison* in question was located just over the hill in Ville d'Avray. How convenient for me. Just over the hill — a stone's throw away. This *auberge*, and I guess we can call it an *auberge*, since it was located along the main route between Paris and Versailles and could be considered a rest stop for the weary traveler, was established circa 1934 by René Charrier, who happened, so they say, to be the son of a *bordel* keeper at Chatenay- Malabry, and a *bordel* is *not* what he created. But I digress.

Ville d'Avray, a picturesque town, attracts artists and writers who prefer to live in peace and quiet away from the big city. Many paintings by Camille Corot, a nineteenth-century painter known for his landscapes and figures, feature Les Etangs de Corot (two quiet forest ponds named for him). While the community is mainly bourgeois, it is surprising that such an enterprise has flourished for so many years. To be sure, there were rumors among the townspeople and, as you can imagine, the local hormone-driven adolescents who fantasized that they thought they saw their teacher entering the lieu one day. But again, the French laissez-faire attitude reigned, as the mores became more and more relaxed.

It became known far and wide as Le Roi René (King René), attracting kings, heads of state, politicians, movie stars, businesspeople, statesmen, and married couples. And yes, even moi-même on occasion, introduced to the doorman by my friend as if I were a regular, was among them. I have heard that this was considered a club, suggesting membership. But I never paid an entrance fee, cover charge, or showed proof of membership of any kind. I was even admitted if I appeared alone, not accompanied by a woman, and was recognized; rather rare in itself. *I had it made!*

It was a large house behind a wall with an entrance gate from the street, on a piece of wooded land. In the *garden*, a large tree supported various platform levels, forming a tree house effect — the platforms were equipped with leather-padded mattresses. The house itself was divided into rooms and alcoves, furnished with leather-padded tables, benches, and *banquettes*. The main bar was lined with leather-padded barstools, whose seats were horseshoe-shaped; obvious when you think about it. A rather thoughtful touch, *non*?

Across the rue de Versailles was a very large antique shop with an extended outdoor display of statues, rescued architectural objects, and facade features along narrow alleys, through which I strolled many Saturday and Sunday afternoons, without attention to the *maison* Roi René across the street. The difference, of course, was that one was a daytime activity and the other a strictly nocturnal affair — no interference one from the other. And while the authorities certainly knew and the townspeople suspected, laissez faire was obviously at play. So who does go to such places?

It was said that even the wife of Premier Minister Georges Pompidou, who was to become president of the Republic, had a special table where she came from time to time to do her thing. While I never saw her, I presume "her thing" was pretty much the same as everyone else's *thing*. But then, who knows?

As with popular nightspots around the world, people go to see and be seen. Some go to participate, some go to watch, and many go to do both. Since the atmosphere is one of *anything goes* (tolerance), it is easy to get caught up in the activities of the moment, but always with tacit agreement from those already involved. The whispered comments from observers are often priceless:

"Que c'est joli ça."
"Mon Dieu, c'est superb."
"Oh la la, regard moi ça …ah non,"
"Ca, c'est le comble de la beauté"

These said while watching a femme d'un certain âge masturbate openly but quietly, clothing askew on a banquette against the wall. And like a grass fire, the sexual excitement slowly but surely spread among the observers, to the satisfaction of all. An experienced FCA, while seemingly oblivious to her spectators, was very much aware of the effect she was energizing. (Just thinking about it and the memories it *évoques* — *whew!*) Those who only came to observe would be swept up. It was in the air. It was undeniable. And it was extraordinary. Wonderful erotic visuals; gathered and stored in personal erotic memory archives, were now everywhere, to be observed, remembered and called upon at will. Fantasies are made of such moments. Don't we all harbor specific memories that sometimes well up from the depths of our being, sending chills and pleasant sensations coursing through our brains and our loins?

Suzy told me one time, "Erotic is with one feather; kinky is with the whole chicken." I find the observation both hilarious and à propos. If you don't have any such memories, I weep for you.

But *helas*, on the night of September 18/19, 1973, that all changed.

That afternoon and evening, I was contemplating whether to hop over the hill to Ville d'Avary and the Maison Roi René perhaps later that night. This was not a place where I spent many evenings. It was special — the right mood, a frame of mind with certain expectations, was necessary for me. I wouldn't have gone before 11:00 pm anyway. Did I know René personally? No, but since he was always sitting behind the bar greeting people as they entered. As was the French custom, one always shook the hand of the boss and gave the usual, "Bonjour, René," greeting.

Paris nightlife began after fine dining around eight to nine o'clock. I finally decided that my mood was just not there. It was Tuesday, so probably not a stellar day for great activity, being in the middle of the week. I finally desisted, maybe painted a bit, listened to music or played the guitar, and settled in for a quiet evening alone.

I awoke as usual, prepared to board the little Rive-Gauche train (Les Invalides to Versailles). The train was quick and practical. I drove to work if I needed the car later in the day or if I intended to stay late in Paris after work. I purchased the morning paper, took a seat, prepared to enjoy the scenic ride, unfolded the paper, and read the headline. *Wow!*

Roi René Assassiné!

As I had suspected it would be, Tuesday was a slow night. According to the news, four men entered and bided their time until there were no patrons left. Discussions turned to arguments, and arguments turned to violence. Both René and Gilberte were shot. René succumbed to his wounds; Gilberte survived hers. The police concluded that the *pègre* (the underworld based in Marseille) was probably responsible, as they had been trying to shake down René's business for a cut of the income or perhaps even to take control of this obviously lucrative establishment. Apparently, René would have none of it. His resistance cost him his life.

It was rumored that the thugs did get away with a couple of books with names, addresses, sexual activity preferences, and phone numbers of regular patrons. But this made no sense to me. The *auberge* was certainly never going to telephone people who counted on Le Roi René's discretion above all. As I said, no one ever asked for my name or emitted a membership card in my name or sent a flyer to my address promoting a Saturday Night Panty Party contest. I was simply recognized and admitted – no charge. We paid for our drinks – that's all. To me, it made no sense for the establishment to even have such books. But then, it was not my concern, and I never heard more.

Le Roi René closed its doors for a couple of years, I have been told. I did not follow the investigation or follow-up by the press, which quieted down quickly anyway. While I saw

René several times and always exchanged the usual greeting, there was no other familiarity.

That does *not* mean, however, that my hedonistic life ended. After all, I had accumulated a group of friends. Remember the lady who introduced me to Le Roi René? She told me of an interesting new dining arrangement in Montmartre. It involved a typical charming family-owned neighborhood restaurant serving classic French cuisine in Montmartre.

But there was a difference – *a very intriguing difference.*

The owners transformed a large apartment on an upper floor of a nearby apartment building, furnished it with elegant period furnishings, and served fancy dinner soirées – by personal reference only. In other words, you had to know someone. Of course, it was couples only, and a typical evening would be twelve to twenty people. Dress code was, of course *trés chic*.

Reservations were made by phone to the restaurant. Check-in was at the restaurant itself. The all-inclusive *prix-fixe* (all drinks, food and wine included) was paid at that time. A call was made ahead to the apartment announcing your arrival, and you made your way up the street to the address. With a discreet tap on the door, a shadow crossed the "eye" in the door, the door opened, and the hostess welcomed you and your partner.

This was not a game for the under forty. The clientele were mature, high class, and loved the adventuresome libertine lifestyle. Eroticism depends on *class*; otherwise, it sinks to nothing more than Formica, chrome and something red and black from Victoria's Secret – sound like home?

The apartment was perfectly set up for dinner parties. The food was catered directly from the restaurant. The entrance was a casual lounge bar with sofas and armchairs, where champagne was served and first-name introductions made. Now was the time to visually evaluate the evening's group. The only person you knew was your partner. Imagine – the atmosphere is charged; everyone knows the purpose of the soirée and has been mentally preparing. Eroticism permeates the air, mixed with attractive attire of everyone and the wafting perfumes from the ladies. *Quelle joie!*

The multicourse dinner was called, and the guests moved into the dining room with its single long dining table, beautifully set with period settings; stem crystal and all. By the time dinner was called, one had pretty well sized up the group. The champagne was working; appetites were whetted. As the evening progressed, subtle things began to happen. The lady in the Chanel dress disappeared under the table and seemed to have made her way to the gentleman with the Hermès foulard. She seems to be ...*yes*, it was now obvious that his eyes were half closed and his mouth had gone slack with pleasure. Now the gentleman in the pinstripe suit had both hands down the bodice of the well-endowed lady in the burgundy, watered silk sheath dress while she was ...Oh, yes, apparently her hands were ...*oh my*!

The tall gentleman seemed to have his head buried under the skirts of the grand dame who had skewed her legs to accommodate him, though her velour skirts still covered his head — at least for the moment. Her upper lip was beginning to quiver as she emitted low, soft, undulating whimpers. The guests were losing their inhibitions. The champagne and wine were having their influence, and the soirée was well under way. Many remained at the table, while others moved to sofas or easy chairs even before dessert was served. It was always understood that the dress code included such details as: Panty hose are a no-no, and panties are optional anyway, while stockings and garter belts are highly recommended — *favored by all in fact.*

Going back a bit to my first *soirée-fine* at this unique restaurant, I was accompanied by my FCA lady friend, who made all this possible for me. Yet we were not actually involved — just "partners in crime," so to speak. But she always had admirers wherever we went so was well taken care of.

As we entered into the bar/lounge and were introduced around, my eyes immediately fell upon my perfect fantasy woman — mid fifties, buxom, blond, and stunning; she was a more-than-perfect FCA. Her eyes (remember *le cochon dans les yeux*?) grabbed my attention, and our gazes locked for some seconds. They told me everything about her in that glance; she was a wonderfully sexual being, drawing me to her like a spider to her web. Pure lust welled up in me; I couldn't wait to get my face between her thighs.

She was Suzy, and her husband; Pierre. Their lady friend was Andrée. This was the beginning of a wonderful relationship. The soiree was a highlight in my *vie nocturne* already, but there was much more to come. I was immediately invited to their home the following Friday — and every Friday thereafter.

Pierre was an architect/builder who designed and built an apartment building near the Ètoile (Arc de Triomphe) to the usual six-story maximum. He kept half of the roof garden for himself, and it became a beautiful, country-style home filled with period French furniture; stretched fabric walls, tapestries, and period art completed the ambiance. The terrace was surrounded by a ten-foot ivy-covered wall. One could not see down over the wall to the street; only the sky was in view. Hardly any street noises reached the terrace from below. It offered total privacy, ideal for the discreet social life, both in the house and outdoors under the stars. Soirées-fines such as I have been describing demand high class surroundings; chic people; fine dress; and, of course, the French language. Eroticism requires a high-class environment. (Chrome and Formica furniture — sorry, but no!) As Pierre used to say "Pornography is the eroticism of the poor."

Every Friday evening, a select group of friends brought champagne wines, pâtés, patisseries, fruit, and condiments of all sorts — a full and luscious table worthy of any Roman orgy.

Andrée, a fine woman in body and soul, was at least sixty at the time, with a noble stature and erect nipples like pencil erasers. She would dress as a variation on the historic French maid — in other words, high heels, 1930s- style stockings (with the seam up the back of the leg), garter belt, a little white maid's cap, and the classic small white apron and *nothing more*. She would circulate with champagne or hors d'oeuvres, accepting caresses and kisses for her service. Of course scenes of debauchery were erupting everywhere, with accompanying moans, groans, whimpers, and cries. And it went on all night. Participate, watch, observe rest, eat, drink, and then begin again. But Suzy was mine, and Pierre was happy because Suzy was happy. He loved to watch Suzy explode in ecstasy.

In the morning, a few remaining friends sat around drinking morning coffee and chatting. Pierre and Suzy vowed that they had *never* cheated on one another. Anything they did, they did up front, in the same room, and always among friends.

A dear friend once quoted a familiar phrase to me, "Happy wife, Happy life."But she failed to add, "No matter *whose* wife and *who is* making her happy."

(I learned from Andrée years later on my way back from Africa via Paris that Suzy died of a brain tumor. RIP, my lovely.)

All of this life I am describing was discreet and private, *not* something one discussed in the office on Monday morning. I did, however, make a wish come true for a very dear business friend. He lived in London. I knew his wife, and we saw a lot of each other over a period of a few years. Peter was the only professional acquaintance with whom I ever discussed such things. He said he dreamed that *just once* in his life he could experience such a night — which is, let's admit it, every man's dream without exception and many women's too, though they are loathe to admit it.

I told Peter to arrange a business trip to Paris for a Friday meeting with me, returning to London on Saturday. I could arrange such a night. I spoke to my friends, and we did just that — a total night of debauchery including Peter. Andrée saw that he was well treated. It was a long night. When I drove him to the airport for his flight to London on Saturday morning, he assured me that, without question, I had made his life complete. *Nothing* in his wildest dreams could ever compare with what I had provided, he said.

(*Shortly after I made my move to Rio de Janeiro, I learned from a business friend that Peter had contracted a vicious form of cancer and died within a couple of months. RIP, dear friend.*)

Un Reve Une Promesse 1996

Le bonheur est infiniment subtil.
Un parfum, un geste, un sourire…
Ce qui fut un jour mon rêve
Devint les délices de l'amour.
Te souviens-tu?

Notre rêve préféré?
Qu'au bout des vingt printemps à venir,
Malgré que les fleurs se faneront, Amour
Qu'en bouton, renaisse notre rose du désir.
C'était dit en chuchotant, comme causent
  les rêveurs.
Vingt ans? Le temps de mûrir un bon vin.
Mais aussi sûr que les eaux qui vaguent
  vers la mer,
Le sablier du destin compte lentement ses
  grains.
S'il en est, qu'un jour les choses tournent
  au pis,
Et que la nuit nous fait languir dans le
  désespoir,
Si moi, comme l'oiseau, ne réponds plus a
  l'appeau,
C'est que Dieu aurait déjà clos mon
  histoire.
Mais ainsi le temps passe, comme le
  souffle du vent
Et les rêves? Mais taisez-vous donc mon
  coeur,
Car nous sommes encore très bien
  disposes

A réaliser notre rêve préféré; n'ayez pas
  peur.

A Dream a Promise

Happiness is infinitely subtle
An odor, a gest, a smile …
That which was one day my dream
Became the delights of love.
Do you remember?

Our favorite dream?
That after twenty springtimes yet to come,
notwithstanding that flowers wilt, my Love.
That a bud springs to life, our rose of desire.
It was said in whispers, as dreamers do.

Twenty years? The time to age a fine wine.
But as certain as water flows to the sea,

The hourglass of destiny slowly counts its
  grains.
If it is to be that one day things turn sour,

And night makes us languish in despair,

If I, like a bird, should fail to answer the
  call,
It is that God would have already closed
  my story.
But alas the time passes, like a buffet of
  wind.
And the dreams? But be still my heart,

As we are still quite capable

Of realizing our favorite dream; have no
  fear.

Chapter 12

Raymond Loewy

In December 1960, I returned to France and took the train that very same night to Austria for the preplanned month of skiing in Hochgurgl, Austrian Tyrol, with Annie. We both loved to ski. So this was a wonderful way for us to reunite after my visit to the United States, before returning to Paris, the St. Thomas, and my beginning a more serious professional life after almost four years of the incredible hedonistic bohemian life I had been living, not that I intended to change completely.

After all, life is meant to be lived, *non*?

I had had enough of part-time work in French architectural offices, tutoring high school students in math, playing guitar and singing in bars and cafés. Now I was ready to get down to more serious work. My French language command by that time was where I wanted it to be — *no American accent*!

So, where to begin to find a serious job?

I heard that the world-famous industrial designer Raymond Loewy ("The man who shaped America," cover of *Time* magazine in 1949) had a design office in Paris. I decided to find it, and I did. Why not begin by applying at the top, though I did not consider myself an industrial designer? I was an architect, didn't really know what industrial designers did. But we shall see what we shall see.

I knocked on the door so to speak, was interviewed, and was hired by the Compagnie de l'Esthetique Industrielle (CEI), Raymond Loewy, Paris. CEI had signed a comprehensive design contract with British Petroleum, London, which would include architecture. And CEI needed someone with an architectural degree and a genuine command of the English language, plus fluent French. I fit the bill.

Mr. Loewy himself was not in Paris at that moment. He spent six months of the year in New York and Palm Springs, California, and six months of the year in Paris, plus time out in St. Tropez where he kept a reasonable sized yacht, named LORAYMO (LOewy RAYMOnd – Get it?). In the New York office, he had a partner, but CEI Paris was his personal pet, and he guarded it like a dog with a bone..

It was a month or so before I met him, and I remember the moment so well because it was the beginning of a wonderful fifteen-year relationship. It was the only salaried, long-term job I ever held. The others were temporary summer jobs. Since the end of those fifteen years, I have been a one-man consulting firm, both in Brazil and the United States. When you are your own boss, you can't ask for a raise. But you can't get fired either, and vacation time is whenever you choose (or can afford it). It is sink or swim.

CEI, an office of about thirty-two employees, counting secretaries, dealt with French and European multinational companies. The three departments handled product design, graphic design and architectural/transportation design. Except for French companies, the others generally used English as the working language around Europe. Many of our multinational clients needed input from all three of the departments, so I became design coordinator, handling the British Petroleum account, traveling to all of the BP operating companies around the world, giving design presentations, and following up implementation programs.

But contrary to similar companies in the States, we did *not* do advertising. In France, advertising was handled by advertising agencies and likewise, they didn't do industrial design – *we* did that.

Raymond; Viola; and their young daughter, Laurence (1953–2008) had an apartment within our office space — an unusual setup. They came and went through the CEI front door so we saw them every day as a family, teacup poodles and all. And Raymond had his office within our office space too.

Besides the Paris apartment, they had their exquisite Manoir de La Cense in the Rambouillet forest, about a half-hour drive from CEI. The apartment was really their pied-à-terre — convenient for Paris restaurants, theatre, and so on. La Cense was really their French home.

Le Manoir de La Cense was always referred to as "the farm" by Raymond and Viola, with several very noisy peacocks strutting freely in the courtyard or up on the surrounding walls. In the fifteenth century, it was but a small hunting lodge, increased in size by each subsequent owner. By the time Henry IV had it for his favorite lady friend, Gabrielle d'Estrées, it might even have been taken for a small chateau. The front main facade was the living quarters. The old route went right through the manoir - in through the front portico and straight out the back portico. While evoking a country atmosphere with its ancient exposed wood beams, the furnishings were a mixture of Louis XIII and Louis XV, mixed with an eclectic collection of comfort, character, beauty and utility accessories, as expected to be found in the home of a modern country gentleman. Completing the enclosure of the large courtyard were the stables and equipment sheds. And at the back, there was a restored café, complete with a huge windup calliope and an ancient shooting gallery. For us, it was the lieu for many weekend parties.

When RL learned that my parents were coming to Paris, he said, "Chuck, we will be in St. Tropez, but you call Jean," the mayor of the town of La Cense and caretaker of *la ferme*, "and work out menus with him, and you and your folks use the farm for the weekend." I knew Jean very well and he received us admirably.

What a gracious gesture on RL's part.

I even remember my meal choices, which I thought would please my Mom and Dad—*lapin chasseur* (rabbit prepared hunter's style) for Saturday and *roti de veau aux endives* (roast of veal with braised endive) for Sunday. My parents, as you can imagine, loved the enchanting weekend.

Raymond and Viola were very gracious, kind people. When I had clients to entertain for dinner, RL would often say, "Why don't you take the Avanti (a Loewy design) tonight? It's down in the garage." His Avanti had a unique plaid interior. I would sometimes use the Avanti, though I'm never comfortable using someone else's automobile.

As design coordinator in an office of about thirty-two people, including secretaries, I learned to accept the designer's intellectual approach to solving design problems, saving my American, more practical approach to problem solving as an evaluation tool at the end. Sometimes it took the designers longer to arrive at a solution, but I never said, "I could have told you so." But their intellectual approach (which I sometimes jokingly referred to as *masturbation of the mind*) allowed them to be convinced of their solution, having left no stone unturned. And they always came up with great solutions, so why should I question their approach just because it was somewhat different from mine?

I was traveling regularly to many countries of Europe, but mainly to London, which was how I acquired the key to the apartment of a beautiful English CFA, who I met when she was running a sweet shop in the West London Air Terminal. I would say she was probably early sixties, but to me she was so exquisite, so desirable, and yet at the same time quite innocent, that I *had* to make her acquaintance. I was hurrying, catching a plane to Paris, so I didn't have time to chat with her at that moment. *I could only gaze and admire.*

I didn't have a phone number or address—nothing but her first name...*Mary.*

When I returned to Paris, I began a research project by phone to London in order to track her down through the company that handled air terminal boutiques and ancillary businesses. It all worked out eventually. I was able to speak to her by phone, and I convinced her to meet me on my next trip to London. Our relationship developed slowly but magnificently over many trips to London, but the culmination — the bouquet, the *fireworks* — she wanted to have take place in Paris. The night she arrived in Paris, somewhat by surprise, she having reserved a room at the Hotel Georges V for our first night together, I had previously committed to entertain a visiting cousin, Jim, for dinner. I chose Lapérouse, my favorite Left Bank restaurant on the Quai des Grands Augustin, and of course, I included Mary and my wire-haired terrier, *Pistache*, who went to my office with me every day and frequently accompanied me to restaurants.

Lapérouse, founded in 1766, was known for its small, intimate dining rooms and *décor d'epoque* — beautiful even from the street; it reeked of old Parisian charm. The mirrors on the walls were scratched and initialed by patron's diamond rings, a historic tradition at Lapérouse. This was certain to become a night to remember in more ways than one.

Jim, a career military sort, was in Paris on a War College mission. He and his military buddies had undoubtedly begun drinking in the afternoon, well before Mary and I picked him up. Mary was stunning as usual — outstanding in a pale turquoise, full-length sheath dress cut on the bias, which emphasized her more-than-perfect figure.

Jim was loaded, of course. Pistache, already well known to the restaurant, was, as always, well behaved. Jim couldn't take his eyes off Mary, and proceeded to do what too much alcohol does to men in the presence of a gorgeous woman. He became a boor while trying to act sober and charming.

We ordered dinner and wine, plus a small grilled steak for Pistache, for which the *garçon* asked, "How would Pistache like it prepared?" To me, this was normal; it happened to me often in Paris, where dogs are always welcome. But Jim thought that was the funniest thing he had ever heard. "How would he like his steak cooked, ha ha ha, yuk-yuk?" Now, besides being high and hitting on my woman, he was laughing hysterically.

We got through dinner carefully, dropped Jim off at his hotel, and Mary and I retired to the Georges V for our first of many wonderful nights together over the next several years. She was the ideal FCA — beautiful and sensual yet totally innocent in the art of love. But she was ready and willing to learn when led gently, like crossing a stream holding hands, stepping carefully from stone to stone. As usual, I never asked a woman her age. If I liked and desired what I saw, my eyes revealed everything I wished to know.

In the early 1960s, I fulfilled a childhood dream and learned to fly, both sailplanes and power planes. Sailplanes are a sport; powered airplanes are a means of transportation, similar to a sailboat and power boat comparison. I began in 1962 on a disaffected World War II airfield at Chartres, home of one of the world's most beautiful Gothic cathedrals with the most famous stained glass windows ever produced.

The French vacation system in those days meant closing the door for three to four weeks in the summer. Businesses did it, restaurants did it, shops did it, boulangeries did it, and charcuteries did it. But the law stipulated that at least one of each type of food supplier had to remain open in the neighborhood. They couldn't all close for the same period in a given *quartier*. The French don't live well without their daily baguette. And why should they?

After a few years at CEI, I had six weeks paid vacation a year. I would use four weeks in summer, flying sailplanes in the Alps for three weeks, and then a week, either on the Italian or French Riviera. In the winter I would go to the

Massif Central for my other two weeks, so I could do both winter flying at Issoire and ski the Mont d'Or—a decision I could make each morning depending on the weather and wind conditions. In cold weather, near the mountain range, we searched for standing waves in order to climb thousands of meters, limited only by lack of oxygen. We were like birds, flying silently on the wind.

I had a small house trailer for weekends and vacation. I parked it on a ten- meter-by-ten-meter plot of ground in a wooded camping area in the Vallée de Chevreuse, about halfway between Meudon and Chartres. The area was also a nudist colony (which the French prefer to call a *colonie naturiste*). It had a swimming pool and bathrooms but nothing else in the way of creature comforts. Why am I telling you this? Because I recommend it as a wonderful way to live, *specially* for children, who are allowed to grow up naturally without our puritanical hang-ups about the human body. Children raised in this way don't peek through keyholes, trying to steal a look at an older sister or Aunt Alice in her bath. It is also a way for us to realize that we are all the same physically, with very small differences, but the body parts are common to all; everyone is at ease. And you know what happens? If you notice a person of interest, which could be a woman or a man, you say to yourself, "I'd like to see her, or him, *with clothes on.*" The clothes we wear express our tastes and our comportment; they're a visual expression of who we are. Naked, we express nothing; we're each just one living human being among many.

At vacation time, we, members of CAPI (Centre Aérien Pierre Issy) took several of our club sailplanes to the south of France, to soar like eagles in the Alps, camping along a mountain stream. When I had my fill of flying, I would pull my small house trailer across France to Cap d'Agde near Sète and the Spanish border, to a naturist village on the shore of the Mediterranean. That naturist village is now, from what I have read, an actual town, with a two-kilometer beach, a large marina, 2,500 campsites, apartment buildings, hotel, shops, restaurants, nightclubs, bars, a post office, banks and ATMs, launderettes, hairdressers, and other facilities. In all, there are about 180 businesses in the village. One can potentially spend an entire vacation or live year-round without leaving the area or wearing clothes, except as protection from the cold.

But in my day, it was just a simple, basic camping ground, with a swimming pool and a kitchen that provided great but simple French meals. We would take a couple of pans to the kitchen, purchase the quantity of whatever we wanted, and return to our tent or caravan to partake of the meal. In the evening, standard dress was jogging suits if there was a chill in the air.

Once a week, Wednesdays as I remember, the Credit Lyonnais Bank would send two or three employees from the nearby town of Agde, with a cash box, a folding table, and a couple of chairs. They would set up shop (fully clothed), for us mainly to get cash for our daily needs at the little market, the café, or the restaurant. Imagine the scene—naked people in line at the table, their genitalia at table height and eye level to the bank tellers carrying out basic banking transactions. The tellers avoided looking up, keeping their heads down and giving full attention to their work. I always wondered if, back at the bank, they argued as to whose turn it was that day. "No, it's my turn to go. You went last week." Or perhaps they considered it penance.

Standing in line at the little market, basket in hand and naked as a jaybird, trying not to back into the frozen food display case, was comical to say the least.

If you can imagine a beautiful mile-long sandy beach with a couple thousand naked sunbathers, you soon realize that everyone looks pretty much like everyone else. It reminds me of a beach full of basking sea lions and is not at all sexy; it's just *natural*. You can shop, bank, have lunch, or just relax naked. Such freedom is wonderful and exhilarating. In the evening, when the sun goes down, it is common to put on a jogging suit, stroll on the beach, or go dancing in the café.

Things began to change as post-World War II Europe evolved. Since CEI had so many foreign and multinational clients, we couldn't afford to close our do or and be unavailable for a month or two in the summer. We eventually had to adopt a rotational vacation system, which did not please many of our employees, accustomed as they were to renting houses in the country or on the coast somewhere for the entire family. But it had to be done. It's called *progress…* I guess.

Following the BP years, and since we had accumulated considerable knowledge in the petroleum marketing sector, we negotiated a five-year contract with Shell International Petroleum Company (SIPC), covering all aspects of their vast marketing network worldwide, with special attention to their visual manifestations — in other words, architecture, product packaging, uniforms, vehicles, and retail outlets. Such a comprehensive, long-term design contract had never been awarded to an outside industrial design firm. We proposed it. Shell accepted it. And it was a great success. The entire first year consisted of travel to Shell operating companies around the world. We interviewed managers and analyzed and photographed what we saw. The orientation year culminated in the creation of a two-screen, three-projector slide presentation of recommended areas needing study to be undertaken over the next four years. This presentation was then given to top management, marketing directors, and engineers from all of the operating companies. I learned through experience that people in these positions will balk at *fait accompli* decisions foisted upon them by upper management; they had to be included in the decision-making process, or we would have had little hope of selling them on our ideas. In general, people will resist change if they didn't think of the idea themselves or were not involved in its development. It's just human nature.

We tackled each area, recommended design solutions; built scale models; presented our recommendations to the operating company managers, then to the marketers, then to the engineers, all down the line, bringing them all into the program. With everyone's approval and enthusiasm we moved on to building full-scale prototypes in different countries employing different building materials while working with pump manufacturers in Germany, Netherlands, France, England and Japan on new fuel-pump designs. After approval for all this work over several years, we produced design guidelines for the implementation of the program. To this day we still see far-reaching visual manifestations in operating companies around the world as a direct result of our design recommendations.

Hmmm. Someone should write a book about it. What do you think?

RL and Viola didn't fly together on the same plane when flying transatlantic. She and the two teacup poodles would leave one day; RL would leave a day or so later. Often, the night before he was to leave, he'd say, "Chuck, let's have dinner tonight." I always knew where we were going to dine, though I can't remember the name of the restaurant. Why there? Because they served *whole* foie gras (*foie d'oie engraissée*), not *paté* de foie- gras, not *mousse* de foie-gras but the entire foie — and *truffé* besides. It was served with lightly grilled *pain de mie* and great wine. It was unbelievably decadent! And RL would order a goodly amount to take to New York the next day. RL agreed wholeheartedly, and stated often, that life was meant to be lived.

The Soviet Union had contacted Loewy years before my time. They had a dilemma. They sought to manufacture goods for export to the West, but their designers and manufacturers were not familiar with Western markets or consumer tastes (and were somewhat opposed to the idea of consumerism as we know it anyway). They did everything based on five-year plans, filling warehouses with often unattractive or unneeded goods. The Soviets approached Raymond Loewy — world leader in product design, featured on the cover of *Time* magazine, with an outstanding reputation in the field. Loewy went to the US State Department to seek approval, but the reaction was that the climate was not good for such a relationship at that time (Cold War and all). So Loewy declined the offer.

Years later, in 1973 when I was with the Raymond Loewy-CEI Paris organization, the Soviet design contact resurfaced — instigated by Yuri Soloviev, head of VNIITE, the All Union Industrial Design Institute. Yuri, the flag bearer of industrial design in the Soviet Union had met Raymond before at Industrial Design International functions in Europe, and they had struck up a positive relationship. It was not an easy job for Soloviev to convince his government that better-looking, better-built consumer products would sell better at home and in the West and that help should be sought from a Western capitalist design firm — a rather *Western consumerism* argument being proposed to senior Soviet officials.

Our contract was, in fact, the first ever contract for *gray matter* (in other words, *creating*, as opposed to hard goods production). The Soviets would never admit that they could not build — let's say, a truck manufacturing plant. But they could justify the idea that it would be quicker and avoid the inevitable red tape and bureaucratic delays inherent in doing it themselves. So they would contract with a foreign, more efficient company to come in and build the whole thing and deliver it *clé en main* (we call "turnkey" installations), a ready-made factory to produce trucks immediately.

This time the US State Department said, "Okay, no problem." We began negotiating a contract, to the envy of the other top designers of the world. Raymond and I and the CEI art director went to Moscow to meet with Yuri Soloviev and the government entity Licensintorg, a Soviet licensing agency. All contracts with foreign companies must license through one of several such agencies.

When we first went to Moscow, we were advised to do our talking while walking in the street—not in our hotel rooms, which most certainly were bugged. We were warned that an assistant, Tamara, who was always present, was a government agent assigned to keep track of the people we were dealing with. And since she was divorced and I was single, it was decided that she was to be *my* responsibility. Every subsequent trip to Moscow, my job was to purchase greatly appreciated feminine items as gifts—things that were scarce and expensive for Soviet citizens (eau de toilette, fancy soap, panty hose, lotions and potions, and more). Soviet women tended to wear wigs because of the scarcity of quality hair products. Easy on, easy off.

I knew of the very old, historically valuable wooden buildings in the Soviet Union. I asked Tamara if she could arrange for us to visit some of them.

Her response was, "Why would you want to see those *old* things, when we have so many new, modern buildings?" I explained that, because of my architectural education and background, I was interested in the history of old structures. She warmed somewhat to the idea and finally arranged a day outside of Moscow to visit small towns with wonderful wood houses and quaint churches.

When Raymond was with us for preliminary discussions, we stayed in the new Hotel Rosiya, which had three thousand rooms, able to house four thousand people. It was not an eyesore per se, just a massive, oversized block of windows located too close to Red Square and the Saint Basil's Cathedral. As was explained to us, when large Communist Party conferences were held, the hotel had rooms and conference seating for all delegates who came from far and wide. Good thinking. (The Hotel Rosiya was demolished in 2006— more good thinking.)

When in the Loewy suite at the Hotel Rosiya, we hardly spoke aloud amongst ourselves but simply wrote notes on small pieces of paper, passed them around for everyone to read, and then tore them up and flushed them down the toilet. If anyone was listening, they must have thought we were suffering serious gastric distress.

I was in my element—negotiating with important government individuals or military generals or CEOs. I enjoyed the challenge, since I was not under *their* control. I was not impressed by their position, only who they were as people and their qualifications.

The same went for my relationship with Raymond Loewy, who I usually addressed as RL. I always told him directly what I was thinking, not what I thought he wanted to hear. He appreciated that and told me so many times.

I was discussing the possible addition of a designer to our staff with RL one day. I remarked, "He seems to be talented." Raymond replied, "Chuck, talent I can *buy*; I want people who can *think*." He was right of course.

Sitting across from Licensintorg representatives was interesting. My impression was that they were professional negotiators—nothing more, nothing less. The specific *product* of the negotiations was of little importance to them. We could be talking door hinges or frying pans; their job was to get the best deal possible. We would negotiate points all morning and then break for lunch. When we returned after many glasses of vodka on their part, they would say, "*Now* we are ready to negotiate."

When Loewy was extolling the qualities of his "great team of young designers, original thinkers full of advanced ideas," and so on, I saw one of them on the other side of the table wince a bit.

He responded, "We *too* have young people like that.... but they are in *Sibeeeria now.* " Ouch!

The Soviets had selected a number of consumer products that were to be redesigned under our contract; things they hoped to export to Western buyers. We divided them up between Raymond Loewy's New York office (Raymond Loewy / William Snaith) and CEI Paris. We chose to redesign the interior of the Moskvich 1600 automobile, a 35mm Zenith camera, LCD and LED watches and clocks, and the Planeta and Saturn motorcycles.

Now the fun of negotiating began. The contract proposal was to be in English, as was all correspondence with the Soviets, which became my responsibility. Their negotiators insisted on many penalties for nonperformance on *our* part but no penalties on their part. For instance, if we didn't present our design recommendations by the contract date, we would be penalized.

I asked, "If you do not get a Moskvitch 1600 car into our hands by the promised date, what will be *your* penalty?"

Their response every time, "No penalty. We *will* get you the car by that date."

And in fact, they always did as promised; never were there any penalties for them (and none for us either). In any case, a contract was finalized, and work began.

I stipulated in the contract that we first produce renderings of our design for the Moskvitch interior, and then we would gut the interior of a real car and do a complete mock-up *in that car*. That modified car would be our design presentation. We would send the completed car back to Moscow, and their engineers would take measurements and produce drawings for production, select materials, and so on. Once the car interior was presented to them, we would have no further responsibility. We would do the same for the electronic clocks and watches. We would produce and present finished designs to them, but we would not work hand in hand with Soviet manufacturers to produce the items (as we certainly would do with our normal Western clients). In the meantime, I was doing research (remember, no computers and no Google back then) for each product and writing what I called "product profile reports" in English, for which I hired a full-time English lady to come to the CEI office and type only for me; only my work. It was a full-time job for the two of us at an accelerated rate, but it worked very well. My hope was that the Soviets would be influenced by my product profiles and would produce reasonable design briefs for us to work from. These reports touched on technical advancements to date, 35mm camera technology, eventual pitfalls for the electronic clocks and watches, sports application of the motorcycles, and what could be expected in the future market or technical trends.

When I eventually sat before the group of Soviet industry representatives (no longer the original "agency" people), I explained what I had done and why, and that I hoped they would take my recommendations into consideration when creating design briefs for us. I held out my product profile reports and waited for them to pick them up and peruse them. Without batting an eye, their leader picked them up, turned them around, gave them back to me, and said, "These are your design briefs."

Wow! What a relief. I couldn't have hoped for a better result. This made our tasks easier. It was then that I awoke to the reality of the situation. In our culture, there would have been many questions from the engineers and marketers across the table, even disagreements, criticism, and tough questions, but not here. In their eyes, their government had chosen us as the experts. They were not about to question us in any way, which would be questioning the Soviet government's judgment. It was pretty much clear sailing from then on. It was now up to us to produce on schedule—and we did.

One of our projects was to redesign the interior of the Moskvitch 1600 sedan. As explained, I proposed that the Soviets place a car at our disposal, and we would design the interior, mock it up in the actual car, and return the car to Moscow. Soviet engineers would produce their working drawings for production; *we would not produce working drawings.* They agreed to this plan. I presumed the Soviets would arrange for the European importer in Brussels, Belgian, to furnish the car for our project.

One day, sitting in my office observing the Tour Eiffel in the distance, I received a phone call from Orly Airport. The person on the line said, "We have a car here for you. What do you want us to do with it?"

I replied, "A car? At Orly? Why Orly? Where did this car come from?" "It came from Moscow on Aeroflot, the Soviet airline."

I said, "Okay. I'll send a flatbed to pick up the car and take it to our model shop." (I didn't want to license the car and insure it to drive on French roads; I just wanted it at our shop.)

The person said, *"Trés bien…*and what should we do with the box?"

"The *box*? What *box*?"

"The car came on a plane, from Moscow, *in a box.* What should we do with the box?"

I replied, "Please save the box. We will use it to send the car back to Moscow, okay?"

The deal was made; they stored the box at Orly, and we got the car to our model shop on a flatbed truck.

If a payment from Moscow was overdue even by a day or two, I would telephone Moscow. The connection was always good until I said, "The monthly bank transfer due yesterday has not arrived."

The response was, "Sorryyy, I cannott heeear you." This was the Soviet sense of humor at work. But actually, *negotiating* a contract was the hard part. Once that was signed, the Soviets did come through with their part of the bargain, and the money.

On future visits to Moscow, without Raymond Loewy's presence, the hotel accommodations changed considerably. For presentations of the electronic clocks and watches, I took René (deceased 2019 - RIP, René my friend), our chief product designer, to Moscow with me. This was in the early stages of LCD and LED digital timepieces, which were very new and very expensive. The Pulsar LED watch retailed for well over $1,000, and you had to press a button with your other hand to illuminate the dial. (Try that with a load of groceries.) As research, I spoke with Swiss watchmakers in Switzerland who were worried for their industry, which depended on piecework done in small factories, even in homes, whereas a vibrating crystal could be spit out of a machine quickly and cheaply.

I made the Soviets aware of two facts in my product profile report — (1) digital watches would be dirt cheap to produce in a few years, and (2) the consumer would eventually abandon the digital face and return to the analog face with rotating hands. Both of these predictions came true. René and his design team produced realistic mock-ups in aluminum and built them into a black briefcase for delivery to the Soviets.

This time we were placed in a hotel far removed from everything, somewhere in Moscow, with massive amounts of snow in the empty, quiet streets. And it was still snowing hard — the kind of snow that muffles all traffic noise. But here there was absolutely no vehicular movement on the streets anyway. The only activity in the poorly lit, outdated, cavernous, cold, gray hotel lobby were several babushkas (grandmothers) wearing heavy winter clothing, up on scaffolding, painting the walls the same sad color as before. At every floor, however, was the ubiquitous stern-faced lady sitting behind a table with a samovar of hot tea; you had to bring your own cup. Apparently Soviets know to travel always with a teacup in their baggage somewhere. These ladies also controlled the coming and going of hotel guests. At an early hour of the morning, piped-in rousing music flooded the room, with no visible way to turn it off or turn down the volume. Welcome to the new day,

Comrade!

Once again, we sat at a table facing representatives of Soviet industry.

After introductions, my first question was, "Did the car we sent you arrive all right?"

"*Da*"(It did).

"Will we be seeing it so we can answer any questions you may have?" "No, it is not necessary."

We never did see the car again. We had fulfilled our obligation, and that was it—no compliments or questions.

I presented the briefcase with the clocks and watch mock-ups, which was greeted with bows and handshakes but no discussion, criticism, or comment. René was perplexed. I explained to him the reasoning behind the reaction. They wouldn't ever question their government's decisions. *We* were the experts, chosen by their government. Their job was to accept our work - no questions asked. Questioning our work would be questioning their government's judgment.

The Skylab and NASA projects done by New York and our five-year contract with Shell International, followed by the Soviet contract, were the culmination of Raymond Loewy's exciting career. Raymond was getting up in years, and he realized it. So did I.

He would close himself in his office, putting together his final book (published in 1979), which contains many photos that I actually took, including the cover photo of Raymond standing in the Skylab "kitchen" and a photo of me talking to RL who is sitting on the moon vehicle. Another photo I had taken (while walking in Moscow) appears in the book. A Soviet had fastened two motorcycles together, and built a body around the ensemble. He pinched in the sides creating what designers today speak of as the "coke bottle effect." RL considers that design as one of his creations and found the photo amusing.

While RL seemed to be preparing for the future (or the end), I found myself doing the same thing. I have a special relationship with this man. And when he is no longer here? He was the strength of the company. He was the figurehead; famous; his name and connection were important. Clients wanted to be able to say, "I met the famous Raymond Loewy." Without him, what will happen to CEI? I remembered my favorite axiom:

A man should change countries every twenty years, jobs every ten years, and women every.....?

Was I unhappy in France? Not at all. I might easily have chosen to spend the rest of my life there. But France and Paris were changing. It seemed that I had lived some of the best years France had to offer after World War II. I was certainly more French than American. I had learned to live with the French, work with them, and suffer with them. Best of all, I'd learned to *understand* them; now I could *love* them. You must get into their heads and look out through their eyes and communicate in their language. Then you can begin to understand them. They are perhaps more individualistic then I am, but I am more pragmatic than they are. I guess that makes for a great marriage, so to speak.

When I look back at photos and an 8mm Christmas film I made years ago, I think we looked like a bunch of kids. Yet we were *creating* — creating things seen round the world. Things that ended up in the Museum of Modern Art collection (the Elna sewing machine for example) of significant designs. And life was exciting every day. The world travel, meeting people from *everywhere* — and it went by so quickly. It was during that period that I became friends with Marie-Luce and Peter Townsend. Since I am an avid pilot and mad about World War II airplanes, Peter wrote in my copy of his book, *Duel of Eagles*:

14/5/1975
Dear Chuck,
It was good knowing you. I hope that great
good fortune awaits you in Brazil.
Good luck and best wishes.
Peter Townsend

We were in touch until Peter's death in 1995.
RIP, Peter my friend

Raymond saw it coming, and now I too see it coming.

He's gone (1986), and soon I will join him and Peter and Gaby and Suzy and Pierre and Mary and Sally and Carole and Annie and Bill and Meilée, and so on. Guess I'd better get back to my writing, *non?*

My business travels with CEI for Shell International (SIPC) meant traveling around to all the Shell operating companies of Europe and the World with sometimes weekly trips to London. I had accumulated keys to apartments in London and other European cities belonging to FCAs who I had befriended along the way.

One day, at the West London Air Terminal, which was within walking distance of the London apartment, after checking in, I saw a stunning FCA in need of assistance. She spoke no English, only Portuguese and French. She explained that she, being Brazilian and loyal to Varig, the Brazilian national airline, wanted to return to Rio on a Varig flight, but Varig didn't fly out of London. It did, however, fly Paris to Rio. Alina was trying to book a flight to Paris Orly on Air France, continuing on to Rio with Varig. I felt it my responsibility to help this unfortunate lady in distress. The fact that she was a classic gorgeous FCA played no role in my decision to step in and offer assistance; that's just what I do. So I managed to book her on my same flight to Paris. We took the coach to Heathrow and remained together on the flight to Paris and to her Varig gate to Rio, all the time in deep conversation. Varig called her flight, we kissed *au revoir*, and she said, "If you don't come to Rio, I'll come to Paris."

Oh my. The stars seem to be aligning again.

Sure enough, within a month, I was in Rio de Janeiro on business, which took me also to Belo Horizonte, with a side trip to Ouro Preto and Brasilia, the capital of Brazil. Of course I found time in the evenings to spend with her. And when we had carried out the business reason for the trip, I added a personal week to the beaches of Rio de Janeiro. The client graciously left a car and driver at my disposal for that extra week, part of which I spent in Alina's summer home in Petropolis — A town in the mountains and a great place to escape the scorching summers in Rio.

It was with Alina that I had an interesting experience. It was a story that would make Doris Day and Cary Grant proud — a story straight out of 1940's Hollywood.

During my extra week in Rio, I was invited to a bon voyage party for a friend who was moving to London to take on new company responsibilities.

The party was being hosted by his wife's parents at their apartment in Botafogo; a chic area of Rio. I replied that I had a date that evening, and he replied, "No problem. Bring her along." That is a typical response in Brazil; everyone is always invited with open arms.

I accepted, and confirmed the address.

Since I had a car and driver available, I arranged to pick Alina up at an appointed time. She looked quite striking, as an FCA should. I gave the address to the driver, and off we went to the party. The address overlooked Botafogo Bay, was impressive indeed. The chauffer dropped us at the door, and we took the elevator up to the penthouse.

When the elevator door opened directly into the apartment, I could see a very large, three-tiered living area. First was the foyer with the butler, next the living room two steps down, and then the terrace another two steps down; and through the terrace, the bay and Sugarloaf Mountain bathed in moonlight. With that, the butler, having discreetly asked our names, announced our arrival to the throng of guests all sipping champagne two steps down.

As we were being announced, the guests all turned up toward us, and looks of astonishment flooded their faces. Jaws dropped, and eyes opened wide, followed by exclamations of, "*Mon dieu, Alina. Where have you been?* And on and on they went.

During all the hoopla, my friend sidled up to me and whispered discreetly, "Do you know who that is?"

I replied, "I have no f_ _ _ing idea who she is, other than her name and the fact that we are having one hell of a wonderful week together.

I was very surprised by it all. What a wonderful experience.

It seems she was married to a Frenchman who founded a successful insurance company. He left for work one morning and dropped dead of a heart attack on the street, leaving her with beaucoup money and properties all over town. She was a member of Rio's high society but had apparently decided to drop off the radar screen. She had many friends at the party who hadn't seen or heard from her in some time and wondered what had become of her.

So that was my Cary Grant 1940s moment.

On an earlier business trip to Rio, I'd met another FCA at the Museum of Modern Art while browsing an exhibition. She was an attorney, her brother was an attorney, her mother was an attorney, her father was an attorney, her grandfather was an attorney, her grandmother ... you get the idea. Our photo, which was taken in a restaurant during dinner, appeared in the newspaper. She did come to Paris, to announce that we would marry and have four children (or was it six?) and ... *Not* part of my plans. *Ooof!* I turned off my telephone bell and left Paris until she went home to Rio.

I began to realize that Brazil just might be my next stop on life's journey. I had never lived in the tropics. The people were extremely friendly. And learning another language would be the kind of challenge I love. It would be entirely new, not a rehash of anything. And it would be true to my philosophy of life in three phases:

Phase 1. We grow up. We get an education until our early or mid twenties. Then we take a job, and the climb up the corporate ladder begins.

Phase 2. We do the professional life—in a practice, in an office, and in various companies until one day we realize that we are giving more than we are getting back. It's called *burnout.* "I've had it. I can't take it any more." "Maybe early retirement is the answer. If the company decides to downsize, they'll replace older people with younger, cheaper people. I'm toast." "I might even be asked to train my replacement. Shit happens." "But I'm still young enough to have one more career."

Phase 3. We take the experience, the baggage we have accumulated, and we apply it to something we've always thought we might like to do, such as consulting, writing, teaching, or whatever else may tickle our fancy. An Industrialist decides to begin a new life and buys a pig farm or a franchise ice cream parlor or gets a real estate license. No more rat race, just something to occupy the days, earn some income, and get out of the house. The wife says, "I married him for richer or poorer—but *not* for lunch."

Since our average life span has increased so much in the past seventy-five years, we can be productive well into our later years. I was certainly entering into that third phase of my life, so why not start in a totally new environment? I wasn't looking for another *job*. I was looking for another *life* — one that would be so full of newness and discovery that I would not look back but always ahead. Throughout life one must always throw out a bow wave, well ahead of the boat. When I paint, the next morning I can't wait to see if I like what I produced the day before. When I write, I can't wait for the next day to read what I wrote the day before or the week before, always looking ahead toward a result. Looking back, living in the past is a sure sign of old age taking over, because we are running out of things to look forward to. Our boat is slowing down... there is no bow wave out ahead of us.

When stuck in a phase two job, after years of climbing *the ladder of success*, one realizes that, instead of gaining twenty years of experience, you've really gained one year of experience and repeated it twenty times. That's when burnout sets in. That's what happens to teachers — repeating the same curriculum over and over; only the students change every year, but the grind is the same. For college professors, it's teaching the same Art Appreciation 101 for thirty years, playing campus politics, keeping the head down, and praying for tenure.

In my world travels, I, perhaps unconsciously, was evaluating countries as a possible next step. I had looked at Japan and Thailand. And then I made a decision; Brazil would be it.

I felt comfortable there. I liked the people and the casual approach. I wanted a new language, new people, and life in the tropics would be a first for me. I made several business trips, adding days, even weeks to my schedule so I could mix with Brazilians, which is very easy to do. *And so many beautiful women.* FCAs are in abundance because Latin men are interested in *brotinhos* (young girls). Latin men are very wasteful where women are concerned; they turn their backs on them just when they are ripening to perfection, but that is their loss.

I knew I had to break the news to Raymond that I would be leaving CEI, and France for that matter, and I was uncertain as to how he would react. So I went into his office and began by reminding him of how he had gone to the United States to start a new life following World War I; the excitement of it all.

He said, with enthusiasm, "Oh yes, it was very exciting."

"Well, I want to do the same thing. I have decided to move to Brazil, " I continued explaining the whys and wherefores of my decision, and I wanted him to be the first to know.

He didn't try to dissuade me; didn't criticize my decision, but graciously complimented me on making such an exciting and challenging decision. What else could he say?

The following is an unsolicited letter I received from Raymond three years after leaving CEI (we had always kept in contact; I had even done some market research for his New York office).

Dear Chuck;

It was nice to hear from you and to know that you are now established in Arizona. It reminded me of the many happy years you spent with us at CEI, of the masterful way in which you assumed your major responsibilities, and for fifteen years!

Your kind of Talent is rare.

In my long career — over five decades — I have known only a handful of men who approached your design Talent, and creative imagination.

I always appreciated the often remarkable solutions you produced for difficult problems and situations.

I wish you success in your new professional activities.

Please keep in touch.

as ever your friend.

Raymond

April 5 ᵗʰ 1978

RAYMOND LOEWY.

RAYMOND LOEWY   600 PANORAMA ROAD   PALM SPRINGS   CALIFORNIA   92262   USA

I had to complete the Soviet projects, while passing my paintings past the Beaux Arts for permission to take them out of the country, building crates for my paintings, having garage sales, closing my apartment, and making travel plans to sail from Cannes to Rio, the cheapest way to go with so much household stuff. I said goodbye to my beloved lady friends, fellow pilots, and families.

I took the night train from Paris to Cannes, after a final dinner with Suzanne, my last French FCA who helped me prepare my exit from Paris. Upon arrival in Cannes, I took my thirteen pieces of cabin luggage to where it would be taken out to the *Cristoforo Colombo* by launch. Ships from Cannes anchor out about half a mile off the Croisette and are all festooned with lights at night, reminiscent of a scene from a Fellini film. What a sight.

I had the day to register and check on my seven shipped footlockers, which would go into the hold of the ship. I stepped up to the counter of a café about to order some breakfast when who should appear at my side but an old friend from Paris; Daisy and her little white poodle. Daisy, now retired and living in Cannes, was a working lady I would often encounter at the corner of Blvd. Raspail and Blvd. Montparnasse in Paris, working her section of *trottoir*. Nothing professional; we just chatted about daily stuff, business, my plans, and other such topics.

While checking to make certain my footlockers had arrived, I saw an interesting FCA sitting on a low wall, apparently waiting for someone. I didn't know if she would be a passenger on the ship or if she was alone — just fleeting questions that flashed through my mind. I verified my luggage, did my check-in, and browsed around the Croisette all day.

Later I was meeting the niece of an office friend. She was coming over from Nice to have a bon voyage dinner with me on the terrace of a restaurant across from where the launch would leave to take passengers out to our ship. We were chatting over coffee and cognac when I realized it was past 11:00 pm and that I should probably go over and check on the launch departure. We walked over—no hurry—and got there as the launch was backing out of its slip.

I was about to miss my ride to Brazil? Really? No,

No. Come back! Don't leave me.

And the launch reversed props and came back for me.

We sailed at midnight.

All coordinated to the witching hour (yes, *midnight*) when the *Cristoforo Colombo* sailed away from the lights of Cannes and the Croisette.

I did it!

I had made another big life change—no job, no language, *en avant la musique!*

When you enter a ship from a launch, you enter at sea level; you don't climb a long gangplank up to the open deck while waving down to your friends, family, and the limousine chauffer who delivered you. That's Hollywood stuff. No, you enter directly into the crowded hubbub and confusion of passengers trying to figure out which direction to go to find their cabin. The corridors are very narrow, and passengers are dragging luggage, shoulder bags, and assorted packages through those corridors. Everyplace looks like everyplace else. And because of the ship's structure, corridors come to bulkheads, so passengers must climb short stairways up and over the bulkhead and then back down—but still in the same corridor on the same deck. There are stairways everywhere, some between decks and some just to jump over bulkheads.

When I arrived at my cabin, which was in the bow of the ship and well below the waterline, I saw there was no way my thirteen pieces of cabin luggage could fit into that four-man cabin. The cabin steward who helped me find the cabin and manipulate my luggage said, in Italian, "There is an empty cabin across the corridor; we could put your baggage in there."

I said, "Fine, let's do it."

When he opened the door to that cabin, what did I see but a six-berth, two- bath cabin with four sinks. I said, in my best French/Italian, "How much could I pay to just let me move into this cabin for the whole trip?"

We settled on a ridiculously low price, and I moved in — much to the relief of my three ex-roommates.

The first couple of days, sailing steerage, was spent learning one's way around the ship. It was after all, a floating vacation resort. There was a nightclub, cinema, lounges, sports, shops, gambling, and all the food one can eat (all included in the price) served in two assigned dining rooms. Only bar drinks were charged to us, but prices were very inexpensive because we were in international waters.

Now, where in hell is my dining room? We were assigned to one of two dining rooms; the second dining room was located on a different deck. Immediately upon sailing, the required-by-international-law lifeboat drill took place; we learned where to report, how to put on our life vests, and other important details.

I was so exhausted from my final few weeks in Paris and not being a breakfast eater, I didn't even try to wake up for breakfast. The cabin was well below the waterline, so there were no portholes — no daylight. I rested and read the many books friends had given me for the twelve-day cruise to Rio.

One day, while climbing the stairs to the deck where my dining room was located, at the first landing, I passed the FCA that I had seen at check-in in Cannes, sitting there on that low stone wall. Well, that answered my question at the time. *Yes*, I guess she was indeed a passenger on the *Cristoforo Colombo*.

It registered in my mind, but I thought little more about it.

In my dining room, I was assigned to a table with three other men, We introduced ourselves of course. During those days of rest, I spent the evenings with a group of Swiss passengers who were doing a mini-cruise from Cannes through the Mediterranean and Gibraltar to Barcelona. They would disembark and fly back to Switzerland — vacation over. I asked Carlos, the young Brazilian engineer and tablemate, if there was anything *interesting* on board. Carlos was in his early twenties, returning to Brazil after spending two years on a project in France, so he spoke French

"Sí, I've seen a very attractive girl."
"Is she traveling alone?"
"I believe she is with her mother."
"Okay, let's go find them."

And off we went, looking into all the places where they might be; lounge, nightclub, cinema, up, down and around. We came out on a partially enclosed deck, where a ping-pong game was under way. Carlos gestured, and said,

"There she is, playing ping-pong."
"And her mother?"
"I think that's her mother standing by the window, holding a cigarette with her arms folded."
I said, "You're on. *Let's go.*"

While Carlos arranged to play the next game, I went over to Mom, recognizing her as the FCA I had seen sitting on the wall. I asked,

"Parlez- vous Francais?"
She shook her head, *no*.
"Do you speak English?"
Again a head shake, *no*.
She was Brazilian of course.

Carlos and Angela (the daughter 18 at the time) and Josefa (the mother) and I became a foursome for the rest of the voyage. Two ocean voyages in my lifetime, forty years apart, and both times I encounter mother and daughter travelers. Apparently, my stars had realigned once more. This woman, it turned out, fell into my preferred age group *and* she was a true FCA but only a year and a half my senior. I had simply moved into the age group myself and found the FCA who would become my life partner.

The rest of the voyage was spent communicating with a French/Portuguese pocket dictionary being passed back and forth. The captain of the ship was obviously interested in her too, but every time he strolled by, which was quite often, he would find us together. He would bow his head and say, "Bona sera," and continue on his way.

The crew members would sidle up and spread their lapels wide to expose wristwatches pinned to the lining, offering them for sale. Whiskey and French perfume, stored in locked cupboards scattered around in locations known only to them, were also offered for sale at international water, tax-free prices. Most of the days were spent around the pool deck since the weather was warm and sunny, gazing at the horizon, and watching the flying fishes play. There is always a breeze on the ocean. Actually, it's windy as hell. I learned that a ship at sea is always being painted; it's a never ending job. I've heard that both the Golden Gate bridge and the Eiffel Tower are similar – they too are constantly being painted. It never ends.

I like changing countries by ship, not by air. It gives me several days to think about the past and the future and to wonder, just *what in hell am I doing?*

When we crossed the equator, first timers were subjected to an on-deck hazing by Neptune and his assistants, which entailed a ritual including chocolate sauce, whipped cream, and a dunk in the pool.

The first land cited was the Brazilian offshore island, Fernando de Noronha, known as a top diving destination because of its unrivaled beaches and warm waters teaming with dolphins and sea turtles.

During the trip, we had exchanged addresses and telephone numbers, though I really didn't have either of those things yet. I would be at the mercy of pay phones on street corners.

Now the Brazilian passengers began to show excitement. *Home was not far away.* But with that excitement came a visible veil of doom and gloom. Because their vacation was coming to a close? I wondered. No. As explained to me, they were grousing because they were about to face Brazilian customs (*alfandega*) at the port, known for being difficult and seeking payoffs. I found that humorous—from happy and fun loving to morose and gloomy at the idea of arriving in Rio. But I accepted it as an introduction to the new culture I was adopting.

Our new relationship was solid. I had landed my lifelong FCA on the high seas, even before I landed in my new country, and I was about to arrive in exciting Rio de Janeiro.

Let the adventure begin.

Epilogue

That was 1975. I began to learn Portuguese with the help of my own private FCA, Josefa, and my adopted Brazilian family — three daughters and many in-laws, nephews, and nieces. Josefa was one of fourteen children, spread around Brazil but mainly in the northeast of the country; a few in Curitiba and a few in Sao Pãulo. The state of Piaui was her birthplace — a northeast region that I found fascinating, probably because of my direct connection with it.

We eventually explored the northeast, which includes the states of Bahia, Ceara, Piaui, Pernambuco, Maceio, and Maranhao, in a VW Kombi (which I spent six months transforming into a camping vehicle). From Rio, we went to Brazilia, Belem at the mouth of the Amazon and then down the Atlantic coast back to Rio, camping out on the many beaches and visiting family along the way. We were officially married in the Dominican Republic and now have been together for fifty wonderful years. I was doing well as a design consultant, the 1,000 percent inflation and uncertainty of investing in a crazy economy and the fact that I was now happily married to a lifelong FCA, it became apparent that the best place for us was in the United States. We chose Arizona because of the ideal climate for Josefa, family ties of mine, and the wealth of high-tech aerospace industries as potential clients for my one-man consulting business — product design and designing printed marketing material for the aerospace industries. Result — our home and my studio around a swimming pool on one and a third acres of Arizona desert.

We gathered and cultivated a large Brazilian community, and eventually I was asked by the Brazilian government to become honorary Brazilian consul for Arizona — a function I exercised for twelve years, finally turning it over to a Brazilian/ American friend. It was a non- paying, time consuming but often rewarding job.

Over the years, I became an interpreter for Brazilian Portuguese in federal and municipal courts and a translator of legal documents for education, immigration, marriages, divorces, and births and acquired a permanent teaching certificate for Arizona Community Colleges (valid for life) in marketing and advertising.

A Sigma Chi fraternity brother and MIT classmate, Bob Temple (1934–2007), contacted me, and we worked together on several West African agricultural feasibility studies, for which I visited Mauritania, Guinea, Côte d'Ivoire, Cameroon, Togo, Ghana, Senegal, and Nigeria several times, using my language skills (mostly French) and *gift of gab* to great advantage. I obtained visas to four West African countries in *a single day* in Washington DC, which would normally require weeks of applications, waiting, and telephoning. I asked Bob how he could have expected me to carry this off?

"Because I knew you could do it," he replied - and I did.

So endeth the reading.

www.ingramcontent.com/pod-product-compliance
Lightning Source LLC
Chambersburg PA
CBHW021630120626
46545CB00002B/474